Introducing English Grammar

David J. Young

Lecturer in English,
University of Wales Institute of Science and Technology

Hutchinson

London   Melbourne   Sydney   Auckland   Johannesburg

Hutchinson & Co. (Publishers) Ltd

An imprint of the Hutchinson Publishing Group

17–21 Conway Street, London W1P 6JD

Hutchinson Publishing Group (Australia) Pty Ltd
PO Box 496, 16–22 Church Street, Hawthorne, Melbourne,
Victoria 3122

Hutchinson Group (NZ) Ltd
32–34 View Road, PO Box 40–086, Glenfield, Auckland 10

Hutchinson Group (SA) (Pty) Ltd
PO Box 337, Bergvlei 2012, South Africa

First published 1984

© David J. Young 1984

Set in VIP Times by
D. P. Media Limited, Hitchin, Hertfordshire

Printed and bound in Great Britain
by Anchor Brendon Ltd,
Tiptree, Essex

British Library Cataloguing in Publication Data
Young, David J.
    Introducing English grammar.
    1. English language—Grammar—1950-
    I. Title
    428.2   PE1112

Library of Congress Cataloging in Publication Data
Young, David J.
    Introducing English grammar.

    Includes bibliographical references and index.
    1. English language—Grammar – 1950–   .   I. Title
PE1112.Y58 1984   428.2   84-4531

    ISBN 0 09 155071 8

Introducing English Grammar

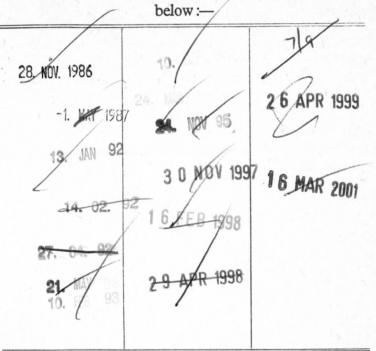

Contents

adverbs – Adverbs as modifiers –
Communicative functions – Indicative and
imperative – Indicative sentences: declarative v.
interrogative – WH-interrogatives –
Alternative interrogatives – Other moods –
Moodless sentences – Communicative function
and discourse – Negation – Voice – Theme –
Sentences: subordination and co-ordination –

Conclusion: structure and meaning – Exercises

Acknowledgements

The author and publishers would like to thank the copyright holders below for their kind permission to reproduce the following material:

Robert Graves for 'I'm Through With You For Ever', from *Poems 1953*.

The *Guardian* for an extract from the issue dated 4 April 1983.

Mrs Annetta Hoffnung for the extract from a speech to the Oxford Union in December 1958, by Gerard Hoffnung.

Preface

In higher education many students are expected to have an acquaintance with the basic concepts that are required for the higher study of the English language, but nowadays such students have often not been taught these concepts. There has been a scarcity of books to which these students could be referred for preliminary reading, since most of the elementary books go well beyond the basic concepts and, in dealing with areas of grammar that are more complex and advanced, become committed to points of view and methods of inquiry that are at least to some extent controversial.

This book is an attempt to satisfy the needs of such readers, by presenting the groundwork of English grammar without going too far in either the subject-matter covered or the development of a theoretical apparatus for the description of languages. I am aware, however, that the ideal cut-off point is hard to find – in fact it seems fairly certain that it is in a different place for different readers. I hope I have arrived at a satisfactory compromise. If the reader finds that I all too often decline to take some matter further, saying that it would be beyond the scope of the present work, I hope he will remember that the work is partly intended to stimulate interests that can only be satisfied by more advanced studies.

A further shortcoming of many elementary works is that they do not contain any discussion of the spirit in which the study of grammar should be undertaken. Popular fallacies about correctness tend to be fostered either explicitly or, more often, by default, so that a student who comes to higher studies often has to unlearn prescriptivist attitudes at the same time as coping with difficult theory. This book begins with a discussion of the reasons for undertaking language study in a spirit of scientific detachment.

There are exercises provided at the end of the chapters, and a key to the exercises is given at the end of the book. At appropriate points in the text the reader is directed to relevant exercises, though many readers may find it preferable to postpone looking at them until the end of the chapter. There is also a glossary to which the reader may find it useful to turn for further help in interpreting technical terms.

There are few notational conventions that need explanation. An asterisk * is placed before an expression that is alleged to be in some way ill-formed or non-existent. I have not included any discussion of phonetics or phonetic transcription, but I have found it necessary in a very few places to provide a representation of the way a word sounds, as opposed to the way it is written. For this purpose I use, for example, /z/ to represent the sound that occurs at the end of the word *his*, and /ɪ/ to represent the vowel in the same word. The diphthong in *boy* is /ɔɪ/. Technical terms are printed in **bold** type when first introduced or when their technical nature has to be highlighted for some other reason.

I am indebted to several people for helpful suggestions, in particular to Mrs Bistra Lucas and Dr Erich Steiner, and to the publisher's own reviewers of my original proposals. Needless to say, I must take full responsibility for the way these suggestions have been implemented.

David Young
Cardiff
June 1983

1 Introduction

Why study grammar?

With many people grammar has a bad name. It is associated with a pedantic insistence on niceties of expression, with pronouncements that some **expression** is 'incorrect' or 'correct' (even though nobody seems to know what 'correctness' is), and with consulting authorities to find out what we 'ought' to say. This view arises from the conception of grammar as a means of regulating behaviour. We start with the assumption that people use language, and then we regard them as misusing it; so we tell them that they ought to be using it differently. It is like rules of etiquette, where we take as our starting point the social occasion to which the rules apply, say a dinner party, and then we state what amounts to good behaviour – or, sometimes, bad behaviour – on such occasions. To look upon grammar in this way is to trivialize it; to take for granted that the language exists, and merely give rules for adjusting the detail.

But this conception overlooks something, and it is something which will enable us to take a very different view of what grammar is. A language cannot be taken for granted; the rules of English do not assume that English already exists and then **prescribe** how we ought to use it. They actually define what counts as English.

The distinction can be understood by making a comparison with the rules of some game, say tennis. A rule which states the existence, dimensions and markings of the tennis court is not a rule which regulates the playing of an already existing game; it is a rule that, together with other rules, defines the game itself. If you play on a cricket pitch, you could not be said to be playing bad tennis, but simply not playing tennis. The rules do not control the game; they create it. Only the most trivial rules have a controlling effect; the most essential rules have a constituting effect.

In order to write a grammar for some language, then, we must study the realities of people's language behaviour and give an account of it in terms of some agreed framework of description. This is a very different thing from attempting to influence people's language behaviour and make them do it 'better'. The grammar that we write will be an account of the structural and functional principles of the language itself. This is no trivial matter, since the language spoken by a community of speakers is one of the most essential factors in the life of that community. The community could not exist without this means of controlling almost every aspect of its life; and language is no less than that. A **grammar**, then, is an attempt to describe the system of communication which every normal member of the community 'possesses' and which is shared by the community at large. It has both a psychological existence within the individual and a social existence within the community.

The term **grammar** can also be used to refer to the system itself. When we talk of 'a' grammar of English, we refer to a book which describes the system. When we talk of 'the' grammar of English, we mean the rules which constitute the language that the individual speaker possesses. From one point of view, the individual speaker is a 'walking grammar' of the language.

We have now moved very far from the view of grammar as fussy and interfering pedantry and can see that it is a serious, absorbing and important study, albeit a complex one. If we accept this view, we commit ourselves to a much more difficult field of study than if we look upon grammar as a body of rules for avoiding solecisms.

At this stage we had better ask what kind of a thing a language is. Linguists have offered many different explanations of the phenomenon. A well-known view of language that has been current recently is that a language is an infinitely large set of sentences. The verbal structures that are the sentences of the language constitute the language itself. An alternative view is that a language is a system for choosing, realizing and signalling meanings. This formulation starts from the idea of an intention to communicate by using such meanings as the language allows; it then refers to the realization of the speaker's intention by his selection of appropriate verbal structures; finally it refers to the fact that the verbal structures must be put into some physical medium – usually speech or writing – in order to be transmitted to an addressee.

It would not be appropriate to discuss these theoretical matters any further here, since it hardly makes any difference to the study of the basic concepts that this book is concerned with. Nevertheless, it is desirable that the reader should see the subject-matter of the book as a step towards the study of something of great importance in the life of human society.

Languages vary

We have spoken of the need to take an objective attitude towards people's language behaviour. This means we should describe it and not judge it. A fact about languages which can be observed without too much difficulty is that they are variable. For one thing, different groups of people speak different **dialects** of a language. We are all familiar with the idea of different regional varieties. The differences are not necessarily just differences of **accent**, but may also include differences of grammar and vocabulary. But not all dialectal varieties are regional. There are also class dialects. A dialect is a variety of the language that is used by an identifiable group of speakers, whether these belong to a region or to a social stratum.

Dialects are different linguistic **systems**; not totally different but partly different from each other. Despite their differences, it is not possible to evaluate them one against another. One cannot compare them for merit. It is worth taking special note of this fact, since it is contrary to many popular notions of dialect. The fact is that different dialects acquire different degrees and kinds of prestige or notoriety according to the social role of the groups of speakers who use them. A group of speakers may be respected or despised by other groups of speakers, and quite often their way of speaking is then characterized as meritorious or inferior. But there is no linguistic justification for such a judgement. The different degrees of respect in which different dialects are held is determined by sociological factors, not linguistic ones.

In using the term 'dialect' here, we mean that the speech of every speaker belongs to one dialect or another; that is, every speaker belongs to some group of speakers who share a variety. We can thus speak of **standard** dialects as well as **non-standard** dialects. A standard dialect is a variety which has wide currency and commands the respect of large numbers of speakers, including many who do not speak it themselves.

Registers

Languages also vary in that the speakers adjust their way of using them when writing a business letter, speaking to a stranger on the telephone, writing an essay, chatting to a close friend, and so on. They are said to switch from one **register** of their language to another. Any speaker who is unable to adapt his language to the varying **situations** of language use would soon be regarded as behaving oddly. Of course, there are for all of us some kinds of situation that are unfamiliar. If we start to operate in new situations, we may have to learn the appropriate way of using language in the new circumstances; but although some people have a wider experience of social situations than others, everybody has some range of experience and some range of language variability to go with it.

Correctness

At this point it may be useful to reflect upon the popular conception of **correctness** in language since, if it is to deal adequately with linguistic reality, it needs refining. How can we judge the 'correctness' of some form of expression without taking into account the circumstances in which the expression is being used? For instance, is it 'correct' to say *smack in the middle*, or should I say *right in the middle*? The informal expression would of course be inappropriate to a situation requiring formality. But informal language is equally systematic, and to equate correctness with formality would be to ignore this. It is obviously necessary to allow that language varies according to circumstances, and what is appropriate in one case may be inappropriate in another. The kinds of factors that change from one situation to another are: first, that the social roles of those who are addressing each other are various; second, the kind of social activity that is going on may be different; and third, the **medium of communication** can change, for instance, from spoken to written medium.

So far we have found two kinds of language variation: there are varieties used by different groups of speakers – dialects; and there are varieties used for different social purposes – **registers**. (The reader should be wary of the latter term since it is also used in other senses and may be a source of misunderstanding; see the glossary.) In general, a single speaker commands one dialect but has a range of registers at his disposal.

Linguistic change

A language may also vary owing to changes that the system undergoes in the course of time. The language of the seventeenth century differs from the language of today. For instance in the seventeenth century it would have been normal to say *I am glad Mr Soandso has made so much despatch*, while today we would probably say something like *I am glad Mr Soandso has got on so quickly*. It would be ridiculous to debate whether seventeenth century usage was more 'correct' than that of the present day; it was just different. Linguistic change is inevitable. Sometimes it may seem that a change has been for the worse. This is because when we are conscious of a change taking place, we are also aware that the change brings some inconvenience with it. But the inconvenience is temporary. When a change has been completed and has become a thing of the past, it is no longer inconvenient and the earlier state of the language system is forgotten; but while the change is in progress, there is instability within the system and people may misunderstand one another, or become irritated by innovations of expression. These misunderstandings and irritations pass away in the course of time and the language emerges from the change neither worse nor better, but simply different.

Let us take a specific example. The word *disinterested* often causes a problem. Some speakers understand by it the same meaning as *impartial*; this is the older-established sense of the word. It is the negative of the word *interested* in the sense 'affected or biased by personal considerations' (see *Chambers's Twentieth Century Dictionary*). Other speakers, however, use the word as a synonym for *uninterested*; that is, they understand it as the negative of *interested* in the sense 'in a state of engaged attention and curiosity'. This is a new sense of *disinterested* which may cause misunderstanding or, more likely, irritation to users of the older sense. It is easy to see how the innovation has come about; the sense of *interested* which is negated by *disinterested* is rather rare and specialized and is probably not very familiar to a good many speakers. The result of the change is a certain amount of inconvenience. When we hear somebody say: *She went to the conference and attended most of the sessions, . . . she was disinterested*, we might not know whether the speaker means that she was bored or that she was impartial. Conversely, if we wish to use the word *disinterested* ourselves, we cannot be confident, unless we know our audience very well, that we shall be understood in the sense we intend. The wise communicator who is conscious of a danger of being misunderstood will normally take steps to avoid it – that is, if the purpose is to communicate rather than to teach his audience a lesson. In the case under discussion there are, after all, the words *impartial* and *unbiased* to resort to. If enough people took this decision, the word *disinterested* might eventually fall into disuse, but this would not matter very much as there are other words and expressions that have come to take on its meaning.

Such matters as these often arouse extraordinarily strong emotions and may give rise to discussions in which terms of abuse such as 'corruption', 'ignorance', 'slovenliness' and 'barbarism' are hurled about. The severity of these words is out of proportion to the very slight ripples on the surface of the language system which cause them. It is sometimes said that writers and teachers have a duty to 'preserve the language from corruption'. Writers and teachers might very well reply that they acknowledge no such duty. In the first place,

change is not corruption but just change, and second, a writer's duty is, presumably, to communicate with his public and a teacher's duty to serve the interests of his pupils. The latter does this partly by ensuring that the pupils are aware of the pitfalls that result from the very nature of language – its mutability. Perhaps teachers who fulfil this duty will be helping to slow down the rate of linguistic change as much as it is possible to slow it down; more than this cannot reasonably be asked of them.

Appropriateness

A language, then, is not a single, monolithic, unvarying system, but a collection of closely related varieties. The notion of 'correctness' that is fostered by popular linguistic lore, and all too often by our educational traditions as well, is too crude a conception to be of much use when we start to study language methodically. 'Correctness' carries with it a sense of rigidity and absolute standards; some form of expression is judged to be right or wrong once and for all. If we replace this notion with the more flexible one of **appropriateness**, we shall be able to save everything that is worth saving from the doctrine of correctness, but at the same time recognize the variability of language. What is appropriate to one set of circumstances may be inappropriate to another. There are no standards of correctness apart from the actual usage of those who speak the language, and these usages are not fixed. (Also see **descriptive** in the glossary.)

The scope of this book

The objectives of grammatical study suggested above are very far-reaching. To describe in any detail a system for choosing, realizing and signalling meanings is a huge task. It is even more formidable than may at first appear since it entails developing a theory of the character of human language in general. One needs a general theory of language so that each language may be described.

In comparison, the aims of this book are very modest indeed. Nevertheless, it deals with some of the most fundamental concepts in language analysis with special reference to the description of English.

A language is a means of constructing utterances (including written 'utterances') for use in communication. This means, among other things, that patterns of wording have to be correlated with meanings. The fundamental concept here is 'patterns of wording'. The verbal patterns are formal **constructions** and the **elements** of these patterns, words, can be identified and studied. In this book we look at certain classes of English words. We ask by what means they are classified, and how they can combine with each other to form phrases and sentences.

Words as formal objects

The word is treated as an element in a formal pattern, something like an abstract shape or figure in the design of some decorative frieze. The reason why it is necessary to do this rather than talk directly of the meanings of words is that meaning is communicated by employing signals, and the signals have to be distinguished from each other by the receiver. Moreover, meaning in language is a property of whole utterances and can only partly be explained by adding up the meanings of the separate words. The interrelationships between the words are crucially important.

Words, then, are vehicles of meaning and elements in meaningful patterns. In the study of language it is important to identify the vehicles and the patterns separately from the meanings.

How do words combine?

Each word in a language is highly restricted in the way it can combine with other words. If you take the words *attractive*, *car*, *cheap*, *house*, *my*, *seemed*, *the*, *was*, it is evident that one cannot choose words from the list and combine them at random. *Seemed was my car the cheap* is not possible, while *My cheap car was attractive* is all right. Some words are alike in their ability to combine with other words: *car* and *house* are alike, and *my* and *the* are alike. This is shown in Figure 1.

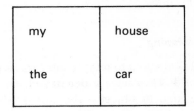

Figure 1

What makes *car* and *house* alike is that either of them can be preceded by *my* or *the*, and what makes *my* and *the* alike is that either of them can be followed by *car* or *house*. When we are looking at the ability of words to combine with each other, we are dealing with their **distribution**. Words that have the same distribution belong to the same distributional class.

Inflection

Many words belong to sets like the following:

> wait, waits, waiting, waited

The first word in this set is the **base form**; it is uninflected. The others are said to be **inflected**. The set of words makes up an inflectional **paradigm** consisting of four forms, one uninflected and the other three inflected.

Different words may belong to different inflectional paradigms. For instance, *cheap* has inflections which are not like those of *wait*:

> cheap, cheaper, cheapest

River belongs to a yet another paradigm:

> river, rivers

Wait, *cheap* and *river* are said to be **variable** words. Such words can be classified according to the pattern of variation. But not all words are variable. Quite apart from such words as *of* and *the*, even words like *attractive* are not variable; there are no words *attractiver* and *attractivest*. If *attractive* is to be classed along with *cheap*, it must be on account of similar distribution, not similar inflection.

Kinds of meaning

Many words are used to refer to our experience of the world. They have a **denotation**. *House* denotes a kind of object – the sort of thing people live in, with a roof and a door, etc. *Cheap* denotes a quality, that is, a relation between certain things; in particular, the quality of being easily obtained especially in exchange for money. *Eat* denotes a dynamic relation between things, a kind of event in which something happens to something. Many everyday words lend themselves fairly easily to the classification of denotations that has been suggested here: objects, qualities and events. *Cup*, *big* and *run* would fit in very well.

There is, however, some difficulty in using these **notional** criteria to classify words. For example, it seems difficult to answer the question whether *cheapness* denotes something different from *cheap*; it could be that the words simply reflect different ways of looking at the same 'piece of reality'. Nor is it clear that all words that appear to be used for talking about the world of our experience have denotations. There might be disputes about the reality of anything denoted by *nice* or *democracy*. It might be held that these words merely signal the approving attitude of the person who uses them.

Since words are formal elements in verbal patterns, and since denotation is such a difficult concept to handle, there is a danger of circularity and lack of precision if we use meanings to identify classes of words. Nevertheless, once the formal classes have been identified by distribution and inflection, it is possible to take note of certain broad correlations of formal classes with types of meaning.

Major and minor classes

In the remainder of this book, apart from the last chapter, which is about sentences, the chapters are based upon the **major** word classes of English: **noun**, **verb** and **adjective**. What is often regarded as a fourth major class, the **adverb**, will be discussed in the chapter on sentences (see pp. 74–7). Major classes, unlike minor ones, contain very large numbers of words, so many that it would hardly be possible to make a complete list of them. When a new word is added to the language, it is added to one of these classes (e.g. *hooha*, *sauna*, *gungy*, *skinhead* . . .). Since it takes a time for a new word to become accepted (if indeed it ever is), the total inventory of words must always be somewhat indeterminate.

Minor word classes are usually small sets of words with a very definite membership: *this*, *these*, *that*, *those* form such a set. There is no possibility of adding more words to the list. In fact, these sets can usually be subdivided until we are left with single words that have a unique distribution; there is no other word quite like *this* or *of*.

The words in the major classes are the sort of words we tend to consult a dictionary about, so they can be thought of as **lexical** items (lexicon means dictionary). We do not usually want to look up words like *the*, *of* or *my*, but only words like the following:

> *nouns* conifer, cupboard, gratitude, partisanship, path, quietness, . . .
> *verbs* appear, boil, consider, improve, represent, speak, synthesize, . . .
> *adjectives* coniferous, grateful, hot, legal, pusillanimous, quiet, wide, . . .
> *adverbs* beautifully, inadvertently, legally, quietly, recently, soon, well, . . .

Words such as these are sometimes called content words, since they tend to have denotations and to constitute the main part of the subject-matter of what we say. Thus the sentence, *My criticism may surprise the performers*, can be reduced to a kind of skeletal sentence: *criticism surprise performers*. The other words, *my*, *may* and *the* belong to minor classes. They are structure words; their chief function is to signal how the content words fit together and fit the context. In some cases they depend on, or are attached to the content words; e.g. *my criticism*, *may surprise*, *the performers*. At other times they stand in place of content words. For instance, in *My criticism may surprise them*, the word *them* stands in place of something that has already been mentioned; *the performers*, perhaps.

Grammar: a technical subject

From what has been said above, it should be obvious that grammar is a serious discipline. Its subject-matter is a particular field of human social behaviour which, even at a superficial glance, can be seen to be highly complex. It is a specialist field of study which, like law, engineering, dentistry, physics, mathematics, logic and history (among others), has its own aims and methods, and makes use of concepts which are not necessarily those which enable us to lead our non-specialist everyday lives. A major difficulty in pursuing such a discipline is that one must familiarize oneself with ways of thought that are more discriminating and analytical than everyday thought. Furthermore, along with the new concepts there is inevitably a technical vocabulary. Without a specialist vocabulary, discourse about the theory and practice of the discipline would not be possible. To the beginner the new terminology may seem like an unnecessary burden. This is usually the case when new concepts are not yet fully understood, so that the terminology appears to be just a list of words which are difficult to remember and even more difficult to use. Difficulty of this sort is inevitable in proportion to the difficulty of the new concepts, but the new concepts have an interest and a usefulness which makes the terminological hurdle worth surmounting.

Exercises

Exercise 1

Here is a small exercise on the distributional classification of words. The words listed can be classified according to their ability to fill the positions in the table. The positions are labelled A, B, C, D, E and F. List the words according to their classes and give each class a number: class 1, class 2, etc. (NB There cannot be more classes than there are positions, but there might be fewer classes than positions.)

a(n)	desk	is	ship
appears	dignified	large	short
becomes	door	moderately	this
building	every	old	untidy
counter	harbour	outstandingly	very
cup	immense	quite	
dark	immensely	rather	

A	B	C	D	E	F
The	new	cottage	seems	extraordinarily	bleak

2 Nouns and noun phrases

Nouns and determiners

In Chapter 1 we talked of the distribution, the inflections and the meanings of words in general. In this chapter our subject-matter will be the distribution, the inflections and the meanings of **nouns**.

It is useful to make a distinction between **common** nouns like *table*, *chair*, *water*, *man* and *poetry*, and **proper** nouns like *Veronica*, *William*, *Smith*, *Spain* and *Everest*. For the present we will confine our attention to common nouns and postpone consideration of proper nouns until towards the end of the chapter.

To start with a few examples, here is a list of some very short sentences each containing a noun. The noun is printed in italics:

> The *dog* barked
> My *garden* was flooded
> This *drink* is very bitter
> A *mistake* has been made
> *Cows* sit chewing

One of the surest ways of telling a noun is its ability to combine with words such as *the*, *this*, *these*, *a*, *some*, *any*, *enough*, etc. These words belong to a class called **determiners**; their structural job is to 'determine' the noun that follows them. Some determiners do this by identifying the noun and some do it by quantifying it. Figure 2 contains two lists. In A the nouns are **identified** and in B they are **quantified**.

A	B
my garden	a garden
your employer	some dogs
its tail	few drinks
his excitement	many daffodils
her prevarications	any mistakes
our course	no cows
their field	enough employers
	much excitement
this drink	
these daffodils	
that mistake	
those cows	
the dog	

Figure 2

The identifying determiners provide a positive answer to questions such as *Which garden? Which employer? What excitement?* The list of identifying determiners in column A of the figure is complete. The first group are personal determiners, because they refer to first, second or third **person** (see p. 29). The second group, *this*, *that*, *these*, *those*, are **demonstrative** determiners; and the remaining one, *the*, is the **definitive article**.

It is also possible to have a noun by itself, without any determiner:

> dogs, daffodils, excitement, butter

Undetermined nouns like these have a kind of all-inclusive or unlimited meaning. *Daffodils are yellow* refers to daffodils in general, typical daffodils; *I am buying daffodils* refers to daffodils as a type of flower as opposed to, say, roses or violets. (Exercise 1 is on p. 31.)

Countable and uncountable nouns

At this point it is possible to bring in a major distinction between two kinds of noun, the **countable** and the **uncountable** (often called **count** and **mass** nouns respectively).

1   Countable nouns   e.g. *chapter*, *child*, *letter*, *pupil*, *street*, *step*. The characteristics of countable nouns are as follows:

   a   They can appear in plural form and can be modified by determiners that indicate plurality, such as *these*, *those*, *many*, *several*, *few*, *a few*, etc. and by any numeral from *two* upwards:

these pupils	a few steps
those letters	two pupils
many streets	three letters
several chances	few children

(NB   It is useful to recognize some expressions as phrasal determiners; thus *a few*, *a lot of*, *plenty of*, *a little* will be treated as determiners.)

   b   Countable nouns in the singular are accompanied by a determiner. Thus the following are not acceptable expressions:

   *He is pupil
   *Letter has arrived for you

   c   Countable nouns can occur in the singular with the **indefinite article** (*a* or *an*) or the numeral *one*:

   a pupil, an egg, one letter

   d   Countable nouns are not modified by the determiner *much*:

   *much street, *much streets

2   Uncountable nouns   e.g. *butter*, *cheese*, *furniture*, *matrimony*, *poetry*, *wine*. The characteristics of uncountable nouns are:

   a   They have no plural form:

   *furnitures, *butters

   b   Uncountable nouns can occur without any determiner even though they are not plural:

   Furniture is expensive
   I have been buying butter and cheese
   He can't stand excitement

   c   Uncountable nouns do not occur with the indefinite article or with the numeral *one*:

   *a furniture, *one poetry

   d   Uncountable nouns can be modified by the determiner *much*:

   We haven't got much furniture
   Was there much excitement?

From the above descriptions it can be seen that some determiners are used to modify only countable singular nouns (e.g. *a*, *one*, *this*, etc.), some only for countable plurals (e.g. *these*, *several*, etc.) and others only for uncountables (*much*). However, some determiners go with a variety of nouns. (Exercise 2 is on p. 32.)

It should be stressed that the division of nouns into countable and uncountable, although valid for a large number of nouns, is not always such a simple dichotomy. There are very many nouns that can be treated as either countable or uncountable. There is usually at least a slight difference of meaning between the two uses. We can think of *cake* as a kind of substance (*There is a lot of cake on the table*) or as a separate object (*There is a cake on the table*). We can say *He is a student of philosophy* (philosophy as an academic discipline) or *We all need a philosophy* (a body of beliefs and principles for living). We can talk about *the discovery of radio* (radio as the physical phenomenon) or we can talk about *a radio* (meaning a piece of equipment for receiving broadcast signals). We must also be aware that almost all uncountable nouns can be treated for special purposes as countables. Even porridge, which is one of the least countable substances known to humanity, can be spoken of as countable if we mean 'a kind of porridge': *This is a porridge which is easy to make and delicious to eat.* (Exercises 3, 4, 5 and 6, p. 32.)

Noun phrases

Expressions in which nouns form the principal element such as *a monastery*, *knowledge*, and *this deception* are called **noun phrases**. A noun phrase has a principal element called the **head** (*monastery, knowledge, deception*) and this may be preceded by a subsidiary element called a **modifier** (*a, this*). This construction is shown in Figure 3.

modifier	head
a	monastery
his	house
—	knowledge
—	skills
this	deception

Figure 3

The modifiers are elements that depend on the head and modify the way we are to understand what the head refers to. The modifiers illustrated above are all determiners, but other types of modifier also appear in the noun phrase. Often these are adjectives, like *large*, *cruel*, *expensive*, *valuable*, *attractive*, *old* and *monastic*. Here are some examples. (For a detailed explanation of adjectives see Chapter 4.)

> his large house
> a cruel deception
> a lot of expensive furniture
> valuable skills
> an attractive old monastic building

In the last of these examples there are three adjectival modifiers in addition to the determiner. Adjectival modifiers come after the determiner when both occur.

Besides determiners and adjectives, nouns too, can function as modifiers to heads. This means that there may be two nouns in a noun phrase, one acting as head and the other as modifier to the head. In the following, the modifiers that are in italics are nouns:

> an *education* policy
> the *house* plans
> *furniture* catalogues
> a *balance* beam
> those *oil* wells

Thus, in *an education policy* the head is *policy* and *education* is a modifier of the head:

> an education policy
> m   m   h

In this notation m stands for modifier and h for head. We can tell that the words in italics are nouns because they would be capable of acting as heads (e.g. *my education*, *this house*, *some furniture*, *the balance*, *a lot of oil*).

Noun phrases may also have modifying elements coming after the head. These are called **post-modifiers**. They may be of various kinds. Here is a miscellaneous list of examples:

> a house in the country
> the house which he has bought
> the men outside
> the people excluded

Only the first two kinds are explicitly dealt with in this book. In the first example *in the country* is a prepositional phrase (see next section), and the second *which he has bought* is a relative clause (see glossary). (Exercises 7 and 8 are on p. 32.)

Prepositions

Another class of structure words that needs to be brought in at this point is the **preposition**.

Any noun phrase can be preceded by a preposition; for instance, *happy little children* can be preceded by *with* to give *with happy little children*. In the following examples the prepositions are in italics:

by the dog
to your employer
with those cows
in butter

inside his largest house
among those oil wells
under a heavy balance beam
through the window

We can also recognize some phrasal prepositions; *in spite of* and *on top of* are among them:

in spite of his deception
on top of the furniture catalogues

Most prepositions denote spatial or temporal relations: *under, over, beside, in, among*, etc. all have a very clear spatial meaning. *Beside the table* or *in the drawer* tells you where to look; *before the meeting, after dinner* and *on Wednesday* tell you when something was. However, they do not all have a spatial or temporal meaning, and even those that do are not always interpretable in so concrete a way:

of the schools
for the office
among other things
in anger
on probation
during the holiday

All of these expressions are examples of the construction known as the **prepositional phrase**. A prepositional phrase consists of two essential elements. The first is an initiating element, the preposition itself. The second is a completer. The completer is sometimes called a **prepositional object** or a **prepositional complement**. The structure can be shown as in Figure 4.

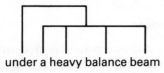

under a heavy balance beam

Figure 4

Prepositional phrases very frequently occur after the head of a noun phrase, and in this position they are called **post-modifiers** of the head. Figure 5 gives two examples with diagrams to show what **constituents** the phrases are made up of. It will be seen that the post-modifier in a noun phrase may itself contain a noun phrase. (Exercises 9 and 10 are on p. 33.)

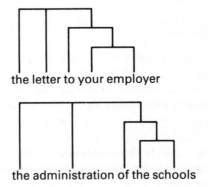

the letter to your employer

the administration of the schools

Figure 5

Inflections of nouns: plural number

The easiest inflection of nouns to recognize is the plural inflection. A pair of forms like *chair* and *chairs* has one form in the singular number and the other in the plural number. Thus the noun *chair* is said to vary for the category of **number**. It is, of course, only countable nouns that are subject to this variation; uncountable nouns are always uninflected for this **category**.

In the vast majority of cases, the noun forms its plural by the addition of a **suffix**, as in *cats, dogs and horses*. This is the 's' suffix. The pronunciation and the spelling are not always the same, but the different pronunciations and spellings can always be predicted. Thus we know that *loss* has the plural ending -*es*, rather than just a simple -*s*. (Exercise 11 is on p. 33.)

Irregular nouns

The sort of nouns just dealt with are **regular**

nouns. They have the standard 's' suffix and this is added to the stem without any change to the stem itself. There are, however, quite a large number of **irregular** nouns. To call them 'irregular' does not mean that they are subject to random variation but that they follow special rules of their own for the formation of the plural. Each irregular formation applies to just a few nouns, sometimes to only one. The following are the main types of irregular number inflection:

1   replacement of the vowel in the stem

> foot – feet
> tooth – teeth
> man   – men

2   replacement of more than a single vowel

> woman – women

(NB In the spelling this looks like the replacement of just one vowel, but in the pronunciation both vowels are changed.)

3   addition of a different suffix

> ox – oxen

4   addition of a different suffix with change in stem

> child – children

(NB   Again the spelling does not reflect the full extent of the change in sound.)

5 · no change at all

> sheep – sheep

6   various forms borrowed from classical languages

> *a*   replacement of *-um* with *-a*
>
> sanatorium – sanatoria
>
> *b*   replacement of *-on* with *-a*
>
> criterion – criteria
>
> *c*   replacement of *-is* with *-es*
>
> analysis – analyses
> basis   – bases

The plurals of foreign origin are often unstable in contemporary English. Speakers of English have a tendency to regularize them, that is, to make them more like the majority of ordinary nouns. Many speakers use a regularized plural such as *sanatoriums*; and some treat *criteria* as a singular of which the plural is *criterias*. It is not possible to predict what patterns will finally emerge from such fluid situations as these; the influences at work often pull in opposite directions. For instance, quite often a foreign plural will be preserved for technical senses (*fungus* and *fungi* in botany) while a regularized one is used for everyday purposes (*fungus* and *funguses*).

In addition to nouns that are irregular in their plural suffix, there are nouns that are irregular in their stem formation when the plural suffix is added. *Loaf*, *calf* and *wife* are among these: they have their final consonant changed from /f/ to /v/ in the plural: *loaves*, *calves* and *wives*. In a similar way, *house* changes the pronunciation of the final consonant (from /s/ to /z/) in the plural *houses*, though this time the change is not reflected in the spelling.

There are several nouns which, because of the accidents of history, have peculiarities connected with the category of number. *Scissors* never occurs in an unsuffixed form except when it is an element in a compound noun like *scissor-sharpener*; for some speakers it is actually converted to use as a singular (*Pass me that scissors*). For those to whom it is a plural (*Pass me those scissors*) there is no singular. **People** is another curious noun. In the sense of referring to a nation it is singular and the plural is regular: *peoples* (*The peoples of the world*). But it also exists as a plural, as in *Three people came in*, and in this sense it has no singular form. (Exercises 12 and 13 are on p. 33.)

Collective number

An interesting phenomenon connected with the category of number is what might be called **collective** number. A noun denoting a group of individuals such as *team*, *class* or *committee* is treated as either a singular or, still in its uninflected form, as a collective:

> The committee is against the proposals (singular)
> The committee are against the proposals (collective)

Collective number is the use of an unsuffixed stem (e.g. *committee*) together with forms that are ordinarily used in combination with plurals (e.g. *are* rather than *is*). Other examples are:

> My class are all very clever; they win lots of prizes (*are* instead of *is*; *they* instead of *it*)
> The team like to warm up for ten minutes (*like* instead of *likes*)

The decision whether to treat a noun as collective seems to depend on whether the speaker is thinking of the group as an entity or as a collection of individuals. (Exercises 14 and 15 are on p. 33.)

Genitive inflection of nouns

Nouns such as *man* inflect not only for number, but also for the distinction between **genitive case** and **common case**. The uninflected form *man* is in the common case. By contrast, in *the man's hat*, *man's* is said to be in the genitive (or possessive) case. The term *case* is a traditional term in the description of classical languages, where it is a topic of much greater complexity than it is in English. For instance, in Latin there are as many as six different case distinctions for nouns. English nouns have very little variability of this kind; we must guard against attributing to English nouns as many cases as there are for Latin ones. This is an error that has frequently been committed in the past because of the mistaken assumption that all languages must be described in terms of the same grammatical distinctions. Nowadays it is realized that each language is a system in its own right and that it has no duty to conform to the norms of some other

language. For instance, in Latin a noun will take one form when it is being used to name the person being addressed – *Waiter!* – and another form when it is being used to refer to that person – *the waiter is coming*. It would be folly to maintain that English has two forms of the noun for these two purposes, a '**vocative** case' and a 'common case', but that the two forms happen not to be distinct!

Case is, then, a category of very limited relevance to English. In the noun, we have just two cases, the common and the genitive. We shall, however, have cause to return to the matter when we discuss personal pronouns, later in this chapter (see p. 29).

Two things need to be said about inflection for genitive case in English. First, inflection for case works alongside inflection for number, so that we have four possible forms:

> man (common, singular) e.g. that man
> man's (genitive, singular) e.g. that man's (as in *that man's dog*)
> men (common, plural) e.g. those men
> men's (genitive, plural) e.g. those men's (as in *those men's dogs*)

Second, it is not so much a noun that is inflected for genitive case as a whole noun phrase: *that man* v. *that man's*. The inflected phrase as a whole acts as a modifier to a head, as shown in Figure 6.

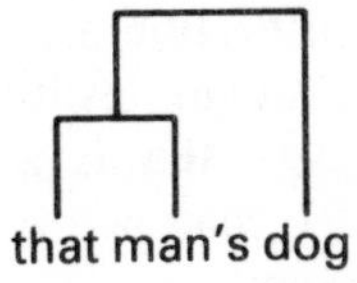

that man's dog

Figure 6

We shall look first at the way number inflection and case inflection coincide with each other. There was good reason to choose *man*, a noun with an irregular plural, to illustrate the genitive inflection. With nouns that form their plurals in the regular way, there are not four different forms in the paradigm, but only two, as follows:

/bɔɪ/	boy	that boy
	{ boy's	that boy's parents
/bɔɪz/	{ boys	those boys
	boys'	those boys' parents

The forms written between slanting strokes represent the pronunciation of the forms. It can be seen that it is only in writing that the last three forms are distinct. It is customary to show the differences by means of using an apostrophe for the genitive forms, placed before or after the 's' according to whether it is singular or plural. People often find it difficult to learn this aspect of English punctuation, since it does not reflect anything in the way the expressions are pronounced. It is necessary for the careful punctuator to carry out a modicum of structural analysis in order to use the apostrophe in the conventional way. (Exercises 16, 17 and 18 are on pp. 33–4.)

An alternative to the genitive inflection

There are a great many nouns that cannot, or cannot easily, be inflected for the genitive case. We would not normally say *that door's colour*, but would prefer the alternative construction *the colour of that door*. The alternative makes use of a prepositional phrase with *of* in the post-modifier position (see p. 29). The nouns that most readily take the inflection are those that denote human beings, human institutions and higher animals; however, this is a very rough rule of thumb, and we shall not go into any further detail on this point.

Another function for genitive nouns

A noun in the genitive case has yet another possible function. It may act by itself as a modifier. In the phrase *a children's department* we can tell that *children* is not modified by *a*, since *a* cannot modify a plural noun. The structure must therefore be that shown in Figure 7. Some expressions in which genitive nouns are used in this way have become established as compound nouns: e.g. *doll's house*, *bird's nest*. (Exercises 19 and 20 are on p. 34.)

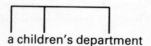

a children's department

Figure 7

The meaning of nouns

Words that denote things (including people and other animate beings) and substances are nouns, e.g. *house* and *water*. This is not to say that all nouns denote things and substances. Our language encourages us to treat many abstract concepts in the same way as we treat things and substances. Thus we can say *three tries* and *not much patience*. But it would surely be circular to say that *a try* must be a 'thing' and that *patience* must be a 'substance' because the words that refer to them are nouns. All we can say is that, in general, the noun is the class of words that is used to denote things and substances.

The difference between countable and uncountable nouns is based upon the physical difference between things and substances. Things are separate, distinct and enduring; substances can be cast into a variety of shapes. Chairs and houses must keep their distinctive form in order to be recognizable; butter, iron and water can be fashioned and moulded. This is all very well for chairs and butter, but as a classification of our experience of the world it is simplistic. Thus there are many kinds of denotation, which, if they are to be squeezed into this framework, will have to be treated arbitrarily. For instance, why should *wheat* be uncountable, while *oats* and *peas* are countable? A large body of small objects is fluid, but each small object is stable, so either way of seeing it would do. Many things can be viewed in either of two ways, both of which would make sense; a cabbage is a stable object while it is growing, but when it has been cooked it is more readily seen as a substance (*I have bought two cabbages; Would you like a little more cabbage?*).

If this is true of some kinds of concrete objects, how much more true is it of abstractions like thought, admiration and deception? *Thought* denotes both an activity and an isolatable item in a thinking programme: *He spends many hours in thought, and then he puts his thoughts on paper.* This is so unpredictable a feature of the English language that it is understandable that foreigners learning English should find it difficult. Thus a student writes: **Road accident is the main cause of heavy expenditure.* How is he to know that *accident* is countable? After all, *luck* is uncountable. Another student writes: **To avoid a terrible damage to the town* [*the authorities*] *passed a bye-law which* .... The error lies in treating *damage* as a countable noun. But supposing the required word had been *threat*, which is not very different, then the determiner would have been necessary: *To avoid a terrible threat to the town* ....

Although it seems that we cannot establish a common feature of denotation that applies to all nouns, at least we can say that they are all suitable for referring to topics that we may want to talk about. Thus they have a rhetorical feature in common. We can say *The bus hit a tree*, or *His industriousness caused resentment.* Here we are talking about 'the bus', 'a tree', 'his industriousness' and 'resentment', all of which are possible topics of discourse. The process of topicalizing abstract conceptions like resentment and industriousness is called **reification**: 'talking about abstractions as though they were things'. This may have dangers of which the philosopher is acutely aware, but it is the way the English language enables its speakers to extend the scope of their discourse beyond reference to concrete objects. Here is a list of nouns taken from about a dozen lines of a text dealing with the history of ideas in the seventeenth century: *date, waning, view, nature, man, replacement, humanist, culture, extent, Renaissance, process,*

century, day, times, orthodoxy, prosperity, stability, civilization, distinction, supernature, doctrine, grace, sin. All of these have a more or less abstract denotation.

Nouns are also used for systems of classification. Fields of activity like commerce, medicine, motor-car maintenance, law, and artistic print-making require that we should distinguish categories of the things we talk about. For instance, talk about print-making requires categories of materials, tools, techniques and products. Some of the words exist only in discourse about this field, and all of the words have meanings that are specialized to it. In a book on 'original prints' the following specialist vocabulary was found. All of the expressions listed are nouns (including some noun-like ing-forms, see p. 44), or are based upon a noun head: *litho-drawing ink, watercolour wash, backing sheet, graver, spitsticker, scorper, burin, mezzotint, aquatint, copperplate, gravure, hard ground etching, wood-cut, lino-cut, lavis, pochoir, photo-stencil, photo-etching, needling, burnishing, collograph, collotype, lithograph, plate lithography, stone lithography, transfer lithography, relief print, screenprint, intaglio print.*

From what has been said it does not follow that all specialist vocabulary consists of nouns; the book on prints includes verbs like *etch*, and adjectives like *lithographic*. But the nouns usually provide the majority of the special terms used in the field. In our age of science and technology new systems of classification are continually being created, usually through nouns that name the categories required.

Derived and compound nouns

Reification and classification require the adaptation of old words to new purposes. Our language enables us to adapt words that are not nouns, like *resent*, into nouns, like *resentment*, and to combine words like *copper* and *plate* to make new nouns like *copperplate*.

Words like *resentment* are formed by adding a purely structural element to a stem. The element -*ment* is a purely structural element; it has no function other than to convert *resent* into a noun. Words like *resentment* are called **derivatives**: *resentment* is 'derived' from *resent*.

Words like *copperplate* are formed by adding two stems together; each part – *copper* and *plate* – has a separate existence with a denotation of its own. Words like *copperplate* are called **compounds**, and the process of forming such words is called **composition**.

It is not only nouns that can be formed by derivation and composition; but it is convenient to deal with such concepts at this point as they are now relevant. We shall have to refer to them several times in later chapters when dealing with verbs, adjectives, etc.

All of the following are derivatives: *snowy*, *adventurous*, *goodness*, *equality*, *organize* and *assassinate*; but only two of them are nouns: *goodness* and *equality*. The words are derived from *snow*, *adventure*, *good*, *equal*, *organ* and *assassin* by the addition of an **affix**. The element to which the affix is added is a **stem**. Affixes that come after the stem are called **suffixes**. There are also **prefixes**, which precede the stems, for example *dis-*, *un-* and *re-* in *distrust*, *unadventurous* and *reorganize*. (See Figures 8 and 9.)

stem	suffix
snow-	-y
adventur-	-ous
good-	-ness
equal-	-ity

prefix	stem
dis-	-trust
un-	-adventurous
re-	-organize

Figure 8   Figure 9

As can be seen, some derivatives come from stems that are themselves complex. Thus, *unadventurous* is derived from *adventurous*, which is in its turn derived from *adventure*. Other examples are: *musicality*, *musical*, *music*; *professionalism*, *professional*, *profession*, *profess*.

Of the words listed in Figures 8 and 9 only

three are nouns, *goodness*, *equality* and *distrust* (e.g. *the goodness of the food*, *such equality of opportunity*, and *his distrust of outsiders* – the last of these can also serve as a verb (*He distrusts outsiders*), see p. 48 in Chapter 3.) There are several suffixes, like -*ness* and -*ity*, which have the function of turning the word in which they occur into a noun. Other suffixes which signal 'this word is a noun' are: -*ment* (replacement), -*ist* (humanist), -*ation* (civilization), -*ion* (distinction), -*y* (orthodoxy), -*ity* (activity).

Further examples of compound words are: *blue-fly*, *half-smile*, *whipping-block*, *copybook*, *witchcraft*, *turnover*, *longwinded*, *understand* and *long-legged*. The last three of these are not nouns, although the rest are. (Exercises 21 and 22 are on p. 34.)

The English lexicon

The **lexicon** is the technical name for the stock of ready-made items that the language contains. These are not only words, but idiomatic expressions like *put down* (meaning 'suppress') and *put out feelers* (meaning 'make tentative inquiries'). The items that make up the lexicon are the lexical stock of the language. Naturally, in the course of history, the lexical stock of a language undergoes many and far-reaching changes. One way of increasing it is to create new words by recombining the elements out of which existing words are constructed. Another way is to borrow words from other languages – **loan words**; in the list of nouns given above for talking about print-making (p. 25), the words *burin* and *pochoir* are from French. In the course of its history, English has borrowed many words from foreign sources, thus acquiring sets of words that have a structural resemblance to each other. The words *creature*, *nature*, *posture*, *pleasure*, etc. all came from an earlier form of French. The ending -*ure* can be recognized as a noun-forming suffix, even though the stems to which it is attached do not exist as separate words: *create-*, *nat-*, *post-*, *pleas-*. Of course we can see a connection between *creat-* and the verb *to create*, and between *pleas-*, and the verb *to please*, but such connections are ghostly remnants of the connections between words in the original language.

Another result of borrowing from other languages is that we have 'imported' certain kinds of compound word. Words like *democrat* and *homicide* are compounds in the languages of origin (Greek and Latin respectively). If we just had these two words, their origin as compounds would not be apparent. But since they are paralleled by *autocrat* and *demography* on the one hand, and *suicide* on the other, we are consious of the possibility of seeing the words as made up of parts. This provides us with a model for coining new words like *plutocrat, bureaucrat and herbicide*.

Thus the lexicon of English is a kind of unmethodical, scrapbook record of the history of the language, and the extent to which it is valid to describe words like the present-day word *pleasure* as having the structure: *pleas + ure* is doubtful.

Even when the elements of which a word is made can be confidently identified, as with *good + ness*, we must still regard the word as, to a certain extent, a ready-made item. It is not possible to predict, from a knowledge of the elements *good* and *ness*, that one of the meanings of *goodness* is 'the quality of being nutritious' (used of food). Similarly with compounds. For example, *blackboard* means 'a surface for writing on with chalk in classrooms'; any connection with the sense of the words *black* and *board* is rather tenuous. Some blackboards are not black, many are not boards, and neither black nor board tells us anything about writing or education. Patterns of derivation and composition, therefore, tend to be partial and unpredictable. (Exercise 23 is on p. 34.)

Productivity

Some affixes are used with great freedom. They are said to be **productive**. The suffix *-ness* can be added to a very large number of adjectives to form a noun: *obvious, obviousness; friendly, friendliness; fruitful, fruitfulness; cheap, cheapness*; and so on. In fact the speaker of English is fairly free to make up new nouns on this model, although he is likely to feel somewhat reluctant to do so if there is an already existing noun with the meaning he desires. For instance, *gratefulness* and *legalness* are likely to be thought rather odd words since they are trying to compete with *gratitude* and *legality*.

Nevertheless, the tendency to coin new words on the model 'adjective + -ness' can be observed when people say things like *sincereness*, if they are not aware of the existence of the word *sincerity* or are unable to think of it on the occasion in question.

The case is different with suffixes like the *-th* in *warmth*. There is only a handful of nouns formed on this pattern, and even some of these have stems that have become less recognizable in the course of history: *width* is based upon *wide*, *length* upon *long*, *health* upon a now obsolete forerunner of the word *whole*, in the sense 'healthy'. In fact, the suffix *-th* is fossilized and almost totally unproductive.

In between the two extremes of *-ness* and *-th* there are many gradations of productiveness (or is it productivity?). The suffix *-ation* is obviously less widely used than *-ness*, but more productive than *-th*. Think of words like *hospitalization*; most words that end in *-ize* seem to accept the further ending fairly readily.

In general, derivation is a historical process that has resulted in the addition of words to the lexical stock of the language over the centuries. It is not indulged in with perfect freedom by the users of English. There are always greater restrictions on the production of new words than on the production of new sentences.

Patterns of composition are also highly constrained. *Breakfast*, based upon *break* and *fast* is an unproductive model. We could not call a garage mechanic a *mend-tyre*. On the other hand, there are highly productive patterns for combining nouns with nouns to form new nouns:

key ring, key chain, key case, key wallet, doorknob, door handle, door hook, notepaper

Since the structure of these expressions is compound, and the process of composition merely entails putting two stems together without modification, it is often not at all clear whether we should count such formations as one word or two. The reader might like to ask himself whether the following expressions are part of his own lexical stock, or whether the model on which they are constructed is so productive that he could interpret them and coin them at need:

chair seat, conference programme, speech therapy, application form, job opportunity, camera shop, floor board, invitation date

I assume that occasionally there will be some hesitation in answering the question. It appears that the contents of one's lexical stock are in some respect indeterminate. It could very well be that the lexical stock and the formation rules for coining new expressions overlap. At all events, the indeterminacy does not affect the 'output' of the language user; he is equally intelligible whether he has 'made it up' or repeated it from memory, and we cannot tell which he has done.

The interesting thing is that a compound expression of the kind *camera shop*, etc. can be incorporated into further layers of composition with results like the following:

key ring wallet, door handle screws, car park attendant, insurance building car park, etc.

This is so fruitful a way of coining new expressions that it is much used in technical vocabularies (e.g. *litho-drawing ink*, *watercolour wash*) and newspaper headlines (e.g. *job loss total*, *cabinet discussion leak*).

Proper nouns

Words like *William*, *London* and *Snowdon* are usually held to be nouns. What is the justification for this? In distribution they are not exactly like common nouns since we cannot normally use determiners with them: *a London*, *this William*, etc.

Moreover, **proper nouns** do not have a denotation; that is, there is no class of objects in the world that we distinguish as williams or londons such that, when we want to refer to one of them, we can construct an expression to indicate which one we are talking about. Proper nouns just do not function in this way; they work by being the name for a given individual. This point is brought home to us when there is more than one person present who is called by the same name. In such circumstances we are conscious that calling by name does not work. We might then convert a proper noun for the occasion to a common noun and say *this William*, *your William*, *the William I know*, *another William*, *three Williams*, etc. In that case, *William* is a common noun denoting the class of human beings whose name is *William*. Alternatively we might introduce more names into the circle of people by calling one of them *Bill*, another *Will*, and so on. The fact that there are not enough different names to go round among the individuals that we need to refer to does not in the least affect the fact that referring to people (and places, etc.) by name and referring to them by means of expressions constructed out of common nouns are quite different ways of referring.

What justifies our regarding proper nouns as nouns is that:

1   they can take the genitive inflection – *William's chair*; *America's coastline*, etc.;
2   they can occur in more or less the same range of combinations with other expressions as can noun phrases – e.g. after prepositions, *beside William*, *of America*, *to Edinburgh* – and in place of the noun phrases shown in Figure 10;
3   they are used for referring to people, animals, places, and so on.

It is of interest to note that not only are proper nouns sometimes redeployed as com-

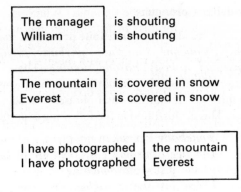

Figure 10

mon nouns (e.g. *this William*), but that common nouns are sometimes used as proper nouns, as in *Doctor will be here in a minute*. We can tell that the word *doctor* is being used as a proper noun in this sentence because, as a common noun it would be countable and would need a determiner before it: *The doctor will be here in a minute*, or *A doctor will be here in a minute*, etc.

Personal pronouns and back reference

One kind of word that can be used for referring to 'things' is the **personal pronoun**. Here are a few examples:

> *I* will be there in a minute
> *You* haven't got much
> *He* is against the proposals
> Please tell *them*
> Show *me* the method

In these examples the pronouns could be replaced by noun phrases, so it is evident that they are functioning in a similar way to noun phrases in the construction of the whole sentence.

A respect in which personal pronouns differ from nouns is that they inflect for a greater number of case distinctions. *I* only appears when the pronoun is the subject of the sentence; otherwise the forms that occur are *me, my, mine*

or *myself*. The choice among these forms is governed by the relation between the pronoun and the rest of the construction in which it is playing a part. We shall not at present investigate these various syntactic relations. Figure 11 gives a table of the personal pronouns in their various forms.

	A		B		C
	a	*b*	*c*	*d*	*e*
1	I	me	my	mine	myself
2	he	him	his	his	himself
3	she	her	her	hers	herself
4	it		its		itself
5	we	us	our	ours	ourselves
6	they	them	their	theirs	themselves
7	you		your	yours	yourself
8					yourselves

Figure 11

The personal pronouns are called personal because they reflect the grammatical category of **person**: first person reference is reference to the one who is speaking (*I, we*, etc.; rows 1 and 5 in the table); second person reference is to the one, or ones, who are being addressed (*you*, etc.; rows 7 and 8 in the table); third person reference is to entities other than the speaker and the addressees, and this includes inanimate objects and abstractions as well as people (*he, she, it, they*, etc.; rows 2, 3, 4 and 6 of the table, as well as *the minister, this tea, Jack, the cheapness of these goods*, etc.). Third person reference can be made by means of either a pronoun or a common noun in a noun phrase; first and second person reference are normally only achieved by the use of a pronoun.

Third person pronouns, *he, she, it, they* and so

on, therefore have the important characteristic of normally being used to refer back to something that has already been mentioned. If you want to know who the speaker means by *she*, you can normally find out by taking note of what female he has just mentioned. This property of **back reference** is not, of course, normal for first and second person pronouns. To find out who the words *I* and *you* refer to, we need only take note of who is speaking and who is being addressed.

When the third person pronouns have this back referring function we can regard them as **substitutes** for noun phrases. In the sentence *He is speaking*, *he* may be a substitute for *my brother*, *the minister* or whatever other nominal group that refers to a male person has recently been used. (In fact the name 'pronoun' might be considered misleading; 'pro-nounphrase' would be better.)

The substitutability of pronouns for noun phrases gives us another criterion for recognizing noun phrases: an expression that can have a third person pronoun substituted for it is likely to be a noun phrase:

> He was astonished at the cheapness of the goods
> He was astonished at it

The second sentence shows that *the cheapness of the goods* is a noun phrase. The same test reveals that *the goods* is also a noun phrase: *He was astonished at the cheapness of them*. So we have one noun phrase within another, as shown in Figure 12. (See p. 21 on post-modifiers.) (Exercises 24 and 25 are on pp. 34–5.)

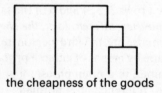

the cheapness of the goods

Figure 12

Indefinite pronouns

There are also a few **indefinite pronouns**: *somebody*, *someone*, *something*, *anybody*, *anyone*, *anything*, *nobody*, *no-one*, *nothing*. These are pronouns since they fulfil the same functions as nouns – or rather, as noun phrases – in sentences. This is illustrated in the following examples:

> *Somebody* has taken my place
> *The vice-chairman* has taken my place
> I have just seen *something*
> I have just seen *a frightening event*

To this list of indefinite pronouns we should probably add the word *one*, which occurs twice in: *One wonders what one ought to do*. The difference between *someone* and *one* is that *someone* is usually taken to mean a single unspecified person, while *one* means any one of people in general including, or perhaps principally, the speaker himself.

This use of the word *one* should not be confused with other uses. *One* is also used as a numeral, contrasting with *two*, *three*, *four*, etc. and with *the other(s)*: e.g. *We saw one house; the others were all shut up*. But there is also a third use of *one* which really is a substitute for a noun (rather than for a noun phrase). It acts as the head of a noun phrase and has modifiers, and can also be inflected for plural number. Here are some examples:

> I have bought a new one (cf. I have a bought a new typewriter)
> This one is too hot (cf. This pie is too hot)
> Have you any free ones? (cf. Have you any free tickets?)
> Some valuable ones have been stolen (cf. Some valuable paintings have been stolen)

Here *one* is acting as a substitute for countable nouns. It cannot substitute for uncountables; so it would not be possible to say *This porridge is too hot; have you got some cool one?* (cf. *Have you got some that is cool?*) (Exercise 26 is on p. 35.)

Determiners as heads

Determiners may be used as heads, as in the following examples:

> *Some* arrived this morning
> I have never seen *many*
> He gave us *two*

Like third person pronouns, these force us to refer back in the context to see what is being referred to. *Some arrived this morning* makes us ask 'Some what?', just as *He arrived this morning* makes us ask 'Who did?'. But there is a difference. *He* stands in place of a whole noun phrase (e.g. *the minister*), while *some* is part of a noun phrase doing duty for the whole (e.g. *some applications*). Here are some more examples:

> I have eaten *both* (e.g. both pieces of toast)
> They have never seen *any* (e.g. any camels)
> *Many* were torn (e.g. many of the envelopes)
> *These* need washing (e.g. these spoons)

The personal determiners (*my, his, her, its,* etc. – see p. 18 and column *c* in Figure 11, p. 29) have special forms for the purpose of acting as head. We do not say **Your is a hard worker*, but *Yours is a hard worker*. The list of appropriate forms appears in column *d* of Figure 11. Some examples in context are:

> I have never seen *theirs* (e.g. their house, or their houses)
> He gave us two of *hers* (e.g. her gramophone records)
> Did you find *mine*? (e.g. my glove, or my gloves)

Most determiners occurring as heads are back-referring. The examples given above amply illustrate this point. However, they are not all so. This is especially the case with *this, that, these,* and *those*. For instance, the sentence *Have you seen these before?* could be spoken while the speaker is pointing to some newly built houses. He is then not referring 'back' to something mentioned, but referring 'out' to something outside the text. This is rather different from the back-referring use of 'this' in *He sent us a lot of information; this was mostly statistical*. Here *this* refers back to *information*.

The technical name for back reference is **anaphora**, and expressions in a text which refer back are said to be **anaphoric**. Not all anaphoric expressions are nouns and pronouns; for instance in *This pub is nicer*, it is a comparative adjective *nicer* that prompts the question 'than what?' (Exercise 27 is on p. 35.)

Summary

The types of noun phrase that have been discussed in this chapter are as follows:

1 *The postman*   noun phrase with common noun head
2 *William*   noun phrase with proper noun head
3 *He*   noun phrase with personal pronoun head
4 *Somebody*   noun phrase with indefinite pronoun head
5 *The green one*   noun phrase with noun substitute head
6 *Some*   noun phrase with determiner head

Exercises

Exercise 1

Indicate with a tick which combinations of words are possible; e.g. since *several houses* is a possible expression, a tick is put in the appropriate box, but the boxes for **several story* and **several anger* are left blank.

	several	those	a	much	most	all	this	the	your
houses	√								
story									
anger									

Exercise 2

If the table in Exercise 1 is filled in correctly (see key) it shows six classes of determiner; i.e. those that go with

1 countable plurals only
2 countable singulars only
3 uncountables only
4 countable plurals or uncountables
5 countable singulars or uncountables
6 all three kinds of head

Assign these determiners to the six classes:

> all, a(n), any, a little, a few, a lot of, enough, her, his, many, most, much, my, no, our, plenty of, several, sŏme (pronounced /sm/ without a stress), sóme (pronounced with stress), that, the, their, these, this, those, your

Exercise 3

Why are the following expressions wrongly formed?

> *three informations; *much library; *several apple; *many carpentry; *enough letter

Exercise 4

Write some sentences containing the nouns *window*, *railway*, *impertinence*, *tea*, *speed*, *luggage*, *roof*, and *grammar*. Where possible write two sentences, using the noun as countable in one and uncountable in the other.

Exercise 5

Which of the following nouns can be recognized as countable or uncountable without reference to the meaning of the noun? (Some of them are nonsense nouns.) For instance, in *my car* the noun cannot be recognized as countable by virtue of the word *my*, since *my* can also be used with uncountables (e.g. *my furniture*).

my car, this reason, his blodge, all carpaw, a lot of trouble, a deed, few sheep, no triss, the information, these honkeri, this herp, their food, much prose, enough hawds

Exercise 6

Identify the nouns and determiners in this passage. Which nouns are countable and which are uncountable?

As I left his house I remembered a story which he used to tell to visitors. He used to say that his parents had been very poor and had not been able to afford much education for him. Consequently he had grown desperate for knowledge and frustrated for want of skills. So he ran away to a monastery where he begged the monks to look after him and teach him arithmetic and farming. Now all this was fiction. His motive for this deception was probably rather complicated.

Exercise 7

Insert the adjectives *wise*, *untidy*, *thick*, *heavy* and *unprofitable* into the noun phrases listed on p. 20 (an education policy, etc.) What generalization can you make about the position they occupy in the phrase? (The answer to this question is not given in the chapter; you should work it out for yourself.)

Exercise 8

Instead of using the symbol m for all modifiers, this time we will differentiate between the various types of modifier. Assign the symbols d for determining modifier, a for adjectival modifier, n for noun modifier and h for head in the following phrases:

your handbag	enough leather
this leather handbag	a lot of notes
some large handbags	several attractive concerts
stodgy pudding	
a sunny pleasure dome	a mystery tour
	much pleasure
bright street lights	happy little children

Exercise 9

Identify the prepositions and the prepositional phrases in the passage cited for Exercise 6 on p. 32.

Exercise 10

Draw structure diagrams like that given for *under a heavy balance beam* for all the prepositional phrases in the following sentences:

> He repaired the machine for a large payment
> The chair beside the kitchen sink is broken
> On your coat there is a dark stain
> Please put the cups from the tray into the basin

Exercise 11

What is the written form of the plural suffix that is added to the following nouns?

> bit, rack, cliff, tab, way, toe, rose, wish, latch, tomato, ledge

In which of the nouns is the suffix pronounced with a hissing sound (represented phonetically as /s/, as at the end of *bus*)? In which is it a buzzing sound (i.e. /z/), as at the end of *buzz*? In which is it as a separate syllable sounding like the word *is* (/ɪz/)? Enter your answers into this table:

	/s/	/z/	/ɪz/
's'	bit		
'es'			

Exercise 12

Do the following nouns form their plural in an irregular way? If so, describe the type of irregularity.

> axe, cactus, crisis, salmon, word, tin, cold, damage, mouth, syllabus, phenomenon, mouse

Exercise 13

What happens to the sense of the following words when they are used in the plural number?

> tin, cold, damage, youth

Exercise 14

1 Which of the following contain instances of collective number? For those that do, note what words in the context lead you to say so.

> The crowd rioted, and were dispersed by the police
> This management has been rather hard on its employees
> I'm going to see a group who play pop music

2 Find an instance of collective number in the poem quoted in Exercise 10 of Chapter 5 (p. 88).

Exercise 15

Listen to a few radio or television news programmes. This is a good source of references to groups of people. Record any instances of collective number and note what it is in the context that enables you to say so.

Exercise 16

In the following sentences some nouns are printed in italics. Decide which case and number they belong to.

> I wasn't referring to those *shoes*
> Three *authors'* works have been banned
> The *lady's* name was called out
> He addressed only the *ladies*
> The *teachers'* room is down the corridor
> The *Companies'* assets have been frozen
> The *Company's* assets have been frozen
> Several *firms'* workers are on strike
> He bought the *girls* hats

Exercise 17

For the following nouns write out sets of examples like those given for *man* and *boy*, on pp. 23 and 24.

> girl, woman, child, baby, wife, mother

Exercise 18

Some of the sentences given in Exercise 16 would be ambiguous if spoken rather than written. For example, the last one could have been *He bought the girls' hats* ('He bought the hats belonging to the girls'), or *He bought the girl's hats* ('He bought the hats belonging to the girl'), or *He bought the girls hats* ('He bought hats for the girls').

See how many ways you could write out the following sentences, where all the apostrophes have been omitted. Explain the different meanings.

> The dogs owner has gone away
> I found the boys books
> She is going to wash the babys nappies in a few minutes
> She is going to wash the babies nappies in a few minutes

Exercise 19

Draw diagrams to show the structure of the following noun phrases:

> a patients' waiting-room, the patient's temperature, the temperature of the patient, those people's car

Exercise 20

Draw diagrams to show two possible structures for *this man's bicycle*. Explain the meaning of the different structures.

Exercise 21

Which of these derivative words are nouns? What suffixes and prefixes can you identify?

Can you think of other words containing the same prefixes and suffixes?

> production, autocratic, existence, unpredictable, capitalism, development, rewrite, friendliness, impossibility

Exercise 22

Here are some compound words. Some of them are nouns and some are not. Which ones are nouns? Are any of the words from which they are constructed nouns? Are the words from which they are constructed simple or derived?

> typewriter, snowplough, overburden, mousetrap, getaway, baby-sit, blackboard, wood-cut, screenprint

Exercise 23

Into what elements can these words be divided? Suggest an analysis and, if possible, find other words containing the same elements to support your analysis. Note any stems which, like that in *nature*, cannot occur as independent words.

> product, progress, ingress, conduct, attentiveness, autocrat, description, possible, defensible, defensibility

Exercise 24

Identify the personal pronouns in this passage. What do the third person pronouns refer to?

People enjoy music from the inside really. I think they enjoy it much more if they can play an instrument, and the proof of this is the tremendous improvement in young people's music-making nowadays. They really are very talented. There are lots of youth orchestras now. I met one the other day and they sight-read a Beethoven symphony. I thought they'd been rehearsing it for weeks.

Exercise 25

The following passage has been edited by replacing all the third person pronouns with noun phrases. See if you can edit it back to the original version.

. . . I've already been told by a colleague at *The Times* that my colleague has already been warned by a source that if Granada journalists disclose the source – the name of the Granada journalists' informant – then my colleague will never get confidential information again from that source, and I'm sure that would happen to thousands of journalists up and down the country.

Exercise 26

Decide whether the word *one* is acting as an indefinite pronoun, as a countable-noun substitute, or as a numeral:

1 We only need one chair. We already have three.
2 One has to be rather careful, doesn't one?
3 There is one biscuit left in the tin.
4 This pen doesn't write very well; I'll have to get a better one.
5 I'll get some fresh ones; those have withered.
6 First he closed one eye, then the other.
7 One can't afford to buy a big one every time.
8 One speaker told the other one to sit down.

Exercise 27

The following are extracts from a leading article in a newspaper on the conflict between the economic interests of farmers and the leisure interests of the public in the countryside. Pick out any expressions that are in any way anaphoric – not just personal pronouns.

The Wildlife and Countryside Act was in part a timid attempt to put the public interest on record alongside that of the occupant. . . . If a farmer wishes to destroy a public amenity . . . it will
5 usually pay him to approach the Ministry of Agriculture and point out the economic benefit of what he is doing. The Ministry will then give him a substantial grant. . . . The Ministry is required by an earlier statute to 'have regard' to
10 the environmental impact.
　. . . The National Conservancy Council has power . . . to designate suitable areas as 'sites of special scientific interest' and having done so it may negotiate with the occupier. . . . But the
15 encounters do not always take place in the decorous manner envisaged by law. . . . In any case the Council can concern itself only with major and obvious sites. It cannot put a fence round every rare orchid. . . . The 'owner' asserts
20 his right to do what he likes with 'his' land. . . . But the public interest requires the gumboot to be on the other foot and the farmer to be advised that he is a trustee, answerable to a much larger body of interested persons.
25 What is most urgently needed is for landscape to be treated as listed buildings are treated. Before any fundamental change can be made, the public interest should be weighed against the private. . . . This would not . . . involve a vast
30 and antisocial growth of bureaucracy. It would simply extend existing protection from one part of the environment (the town) to another (the country). Without such protection anyone with an eye to the disappearing beauties of the
35 English landscape is almost powerless.

(The *Guardian*, 4 April 1983)

3 Verbs and verb phrases

Verbs and their subjects

In Chapter 2 we identified a set of words called personal pronouns (see p. 29) which distinguish between first person (*I*, *we*), second person (*you*) and third person (*he, she, it, they*). (Most of the pronouns also have other forms, *me*, *us*, *him*, etc., but for now we only need to use those in the first column of Figure 11, p. 29.)

The class of words that we are now going to investigate is **verbs**. These are most easily identified by their power of combining with personal pronouns to form a particular kind of construction:

run	She falls
You disappear	He disappears
They cough	It barks
We try	

The words that follow the personal pronoun in these examples are verbs. It will be noticed that they vary in form. When a third person singular pronoun is used the verb takes a suffix '-s', as in *disappears*, *falls* and *barks*. The resulting construction, with the pronoun and the verb combined, has the **force** of a statement. This construction is called the **subject–verb** construction. Such an expression as *I run* has *I* as subject and *run* as verb. When such an expression is uttered, the utterance has a **truth value**; that is to say, the speaker is making a claim. It would make sense to respond with *That's true*; *Yes,*

I know; *Are you sure? That's a lie*; or *How interesting!*

Thus the subject–verb construction differs in a fundamental way from the expressions *we drivers*, *you boys*, *he alone*, etc., which do not by themselves have any communicative force. If somebody utters *we drivers*, we need to wait for him to say something else before we can tell whether he is making a statement or not; it would not be sensible to respond by saying *It isn't true*. (Exercise 1 is on p. 49.)

Verbs with noun-phrase subjects

We have now established one of the most important properties of verbs. They can have subjects. But as yet we have taken a rather limited view of subjects. When the subject is an instance of third person reference (*he, she, it, they*), we could use a more explicit form of words to indicate what we are talking about. Instead of *It barks*, *They sing*, or *She sparkles*, we could say *The dog barks*, *Your friendly neighbours sing*, or *The hostess sparkles*; in fact, very frequently we need to do this to be clear.

Thus we can use a noun phrase with a common noun head as subject. It is clear that *The dog barks* and *The hostess sparkles* are expressions that have a truth value exactly like the expressions that have a personal pronoun as subject. By itself, the expression *the dog* cannot be interpreted as making a claim; all we could say in response is something like *What about it?* At the very least, the utterance of the words *the dog* would have to be accompanied by a gesture such as pointing. But when somebody says *the dog barks*, we know that he is making a claim even without a gesture: the force is conveyed by the words alone.

Verbs and tense

Another peculiarity of verbs is that they can be inflected for **tense**. The most essential tense distinction in English is **present tense** v. **past tense**. All the subject–verb expressions listed so far are in the present tense; but for every one of them there is a corresponding past tense:

The dog barks	The dog barked
They sing	They sang
You disappear	You disappeared
The trees grow	The trees grew

The chief use of the past tense is to talk about situations that are over and done with, no longer existent or relevant. We shall have more to say about tense and the inflection of verbs shortly. (Exercise 2 is on p. 49.)

Verbs and their complements

The examples given above are obviously extremely simple ones. In the vast majority of utterances there is more than just a subject and a verb. There is usually at least one further element to complete or supplement the construction. The total range of construction types for whole sentences is very great; a slightly fuller treatment of the topic will be found in Chapter 5 (see pp. 71–4). However, it is necessary to anticipate a little of this material, since it will help us to understand the distribution of verbs.

Some verbs need to be followed by a completing element. The technical name for such an element is **complement**. For instance, we would not normally say, *he mentioned* or *the tank seems*. *Mention* and *seem* are verbs that take a complement, so we would expect them to occur in sentences like the following:

> He mentioned the evidence
> The tank seems empty

In these sentences *the evidence* and *empty* are complements.

Other verbs, however, occur very readily without any complement. In the following list of examples the verb occurs either without anything to follow it, or with an optional addition. The technical name for optional additions is **adjunct**. The difference between adjuncts and complements is that complements are essential to the structure of the sentence while adjuncts are not; adjuncts can easily be omitted without creating a feeling that something has been left unsaid. In these examples the adjuncts are in italics:

> The tree fell
> The boat sailed *early*
> Somebody spoke *for a few minutes*

The verbs *fall*, *sail* and *speak* frequently occur as here without any complement. In the second example *early* is an adjunct. So is *for a few minutes* in the last example.

The difference between complements and adjuncts can be further illustrated by using an ambiguous example. The following sentence has two interpretations:

> He explained last night

In one interpretation, *last night* is a complement; 'it was last night that was explained by him'. In the other interpretation, he explained something, but we are not told what. In this interpretation *last night* says WHEN he explained it, not WHAT he explained. If there had been both a complement and an adjunct in the sentence, the ambiguity would not have arisen:

> He explained last night this morning
> He explained the method last night

In the first example, *last night* is the complement and *this morning* is the adjunct; in the second, *the method* is the complement and *last night* is the adjunct. (Exercise 3 is on p. 49.)

Verb phrases

The 'verb' element in a sentence is not necessarily just a single word. It would be more satisfactory to call it a **verb phrase**, which may be just one verb, or may be made up of several verbs. The examples given above have just one verb in the verb phrase: e.g. *barks*, *disappeared*, *explained*, but in the following the verb phrases contain two or more verbs:

> My landlady has been cooking
> Beetles were crawling
> The ship has disappeared

The verb phrases here are *has been cooking*, *were crawling* and *has disappeared*. *Were crawling* is in the past tense; the others are in the present tense. (It is the first word that signals the choice of tense, *has* v. *had*, *are* v. *were*, *explain* v. *explained*, etc.)

The last verb in a verb phrase is the **main verb**. The words that precede the main verb, if any, are **auxiliary verbs**. In the examples cited just above, the auxiliary verbs are *has been*, *were* and *has* respectively.

The main verb is the most essential part of the construction; it is the word, if there is one, that has denotative meaning. Furthermore, it is the element in the verb phrase that is obligatorily present. So, if there is only one word, it has to be the main verb. The only exception to this statement is when the construction is deliberately left incomplete. For example,

> A I didn't know John had finished
> B Well, he has

An expression like *He has*, which is left incomplete and has to be interpreted by reference to the verbal context, is said to be **elliptical**. (It is an instance of **ellipsis**.) Here, of course, the verb phrase *has* contains no main verb but, all the same, a main verb is an obligatory element in the interpretation of the construction.

Auxiliary verbs, in contrast to main verbs, are subsidiary to the main verb and they contribute special kinds of grammatical meaning (see the next section).

Figure 13 gives some idea of the range of combinations of verbs that make up verb phrases. It is not an exhaustive display of possible types of verb phrase, but it is sufficient for present purposes. The numbers and letters in Figure 13 are referred to below (pp. 39–40).

	A	B	C
1a	grow		
	have	grown	
	have	been	growing
1b	are		growing
	am		growing
2	grows		
	has	grown	
	has	been	growing
	is		growing
3a	grew		
	had	grown	
	had	been	growing
3b	was		growing
	were		growing

Figure 13

Inflections of verbs

Further facts about the distribution of verbs will be presented later. Meanwhile, we need to survey the variations in verb forms. The typical verb has an inflectional paradigm consisting of either four or five forms. (There are also a few atypical verbs which we shall come to shortly.) Here are some examples:

fix	fixes	fixed	fixed	fixing
grow	grows	grew	grown	growing

The first item in each of these lists (*fix*, *grow*) is the **base form**; the others are inflected. The actual changes from the base form to the inflected forms are different in the two lists.

The pattern of variation shown in the top list is that which occurs for the vast majority of English verbs. For this reason it is known as the **regular** pattern, and the verbs that inflect like this are called *regular verbs*. In the regular pattern there is no difference between the third and the fourth items. If all verbs were like this, there would be no point in setting up a paradigm of five forms. But since, with many verbs, there is a real distinction between the third and the fourth items (e.g. *grew* and *grown*), it is simpler to assume a potential difference at this point for all verbs and then to say that the potential is not realized with regular verbs. It was in consideration of this complication that it was said above that most verbs have 'either four or five' forms.

At this point it will be useful to provide names for the five forms in the inflectional paradigm. These can be found in Figure 14.

base form	s-form	d-form	n-form	ing-form
look	looks	looked	looked	looking
take	takes	took	taken	taking

Figure 14

Regular verbs always form their inflected forms by means of adding the standard suffixes to an unvarying stem. Further examples of regular verbs are:

try	tries	tried	tried	trying
skid	skids	skidded	skidded	skidding

Although there are various minor complexities about the spelling and the spoken forms of these words, they are all perfectly predictable – for instance, the change from *try* to *tri-* or from *skid* to *skidd-*, or the different spoken forms of the suffixes in *tries* (with a /z/ sound) and *looks* (with an /s/ sound). These are automatic adjustments of the basic elements.

But **irregular** inflected forms are quite different. Either the stem itself is changed, or the suffix is not the regular suffix, or both. There are a large number of different patterns of irregularity. Here are a few more:

hide	hides	hid	hidden	hiding
go	goes	went	gone	going
hit	hits	hit	hit	hitting
read	reads	read	read	reading
have	has	had	had	having
break	breaks	broke	broken	breaking

It can be seen that most of the irregularity comes in the d-forms and the n-forms. In all verbs the ing-form is regular, and in most verbs (though not *have*) the s-form is regular. In some cases the d- and n-forms are the same as each other, and in some they are different. In some – but not all – cases they differ from the base. But they are all different from the regular forms, which would be: **hided*, **goed*, **hitted*, **readed*, **haved* and **breaked*.

The table in Figure 13 (p. 38) provides a convenient means of checking the identity of the inflected forms of the verbs. Column C has the ing-forms and column B the n-forms. It can be seen that the ing-forms follow the verb *be* which is used as an auxiliary verb. A verb phrase which has these features is called **continuous** (or **progressive**). The n-forms follow the verb *have* used as an auxiliary. Such verb phrases are called **perfect**. Thus, *is growing* is continuous; *has grown* is perfect; and *has been growing* is perfect continuous.

Column A contains all the forms that are required for making the tense of the verb phrase past or present. There are, however, some complications over the verb *be*. These will be dealt with as we come to them.

Column A, section 1*a*, contains the base form of the verbs. If there is no auxiliary, the form shown is the base form of the main verb; otherwise it is the base form of an auxiliary. The base form of the main or auxiliary verb is used in the present tense when the subject is not the third person singular:

present   they (I, we, you) grow

present perfect   they (I, we, you) have grown

present perfect continuous   they (I, we, you) have been growing

Column A, 1*b* has the verb *be* which, however, does not appear in its base form but has two extra forms (*am* and *are*):

present continuous   they (we, you) are growing; I am growing

Column A, 2 has the s-forms of the verbs. This is used for the present tense when the subject is the third person singular:

present   he (she, it) grows

present perfect   he (she, it) has grown

present perfect continuous   he (she, it) has been growing

present continuous   he (she, it) is growing

This time the verb *be* presents no problem since it has an s-form (*is*) that is used like the s-form of other verbs.

Column A, 3 has the forms that are required to make the past tense, namely, the d-form. A, 3*a* has the forms for verbs other than *be*:

past   he (she, it, they, I, we, you) grew

past perfect   he (she, it, they, I, we, you) had grown

past perfect continuous   he (she, it, they, I, we, you) had been growing

Here it can be seen that the choice of subject makes no difference to the form of the verb.

Column A, 3*b* again shows a complication with the verb *be*, which has two d-forms, *was* and *were*, one for first and third person singular subjects, and one for second person and plural subjects:

past continuous   I (he, she, it) was growing; you (they, we) were growing

The table in Figure 13, then, shows the main verb *grow* in its five forms: *grow*, *grows*, *grew*, *grown* and *growing*. It provides a paradigm for the verb phrase and a means of checking on the forms of other verbs, e.g. *think*, *thinks*, *thought*, *thought* and *thinking*.

There are quite a large number of things that the table does not show, however. Some of these will be dealt with shortly. They include:
1   modal verbs;
2   the difference between finite and non-finite verbs;
3   passive voice.
(Exercises 4, 5 and 6 are on pp. 50–1.)

Modal verbs

There is a small and rather special set of verbs called **modal verbs**. These are *may*, *might*, *can*, *could*, *will*, *would*, *shall*, *should*, *must*, *ought*, *need*, and a few others.

The distributional test, that was described on pp. 36–7 above, shows that they are verbs because they can combine with a subject:

They can sing
He may arrive tomorrow
I must have lost my presence of mind
The children can sing
James may arrive tomorrow

Although these words are verbs, they have a much more restricted distribution than most verbs. For one thing, they are always followed by another verb. In the above examples *can* is followed by *sing*, *may* by *arrive*, and *must* by *have* (which, in its turn, is followed by *lost*).

Modal verbs have a maximum of two forms; a base form and an irregular d-form. *Might* is the d-form of *may*; *could* is the d-form of *can*; *would* is the d-form of *will*; and *should* is the d-form of *shall*. But *must*, *ought* and *need* have no d-forms; and none of the modal verbs have s-forms or ing-forms (*mays, *musting, etc.).

Modal verbs always come first in the verb phrase: *may arrive*, *can sing*, *ought to have tried*, etc. The verb *ought* is followed by the **to-infinitive** of the following verb, but this is exceptional; the other modal verbs are all followed by the base form of the next word. Thus we can have *might have* but not *might has* or *might had*, and we can have *can be* but not *can is* or *can was*, etc. This is one of the places where the base form of *be* is used: *He may be arriving tomorrow*.

All the categories of verb phrase that appear in Figure 13 can have a modal verb included in them but, of course, there are not so many variations because the modal verb does not have an s-form. The set of forms for modal verb phrases is the subject of Exercise 7 (on p. 51).

Finite and non-finite verbs

All the sentences we have looked at so far in this chapter have been short and simple statements. They have had a subject and a verb, and sometimes other things following the verb. On p. 36 we described such constructions as having a truth value; they can be true or false.

We must now make a distinction between such constructions as these and another type. The type we started with are called **finite** and the type with which we are now about to contrast them are called **non-finite**. Before attempting a description of the difference, let us look at a few contrasting examples. In the following the first example in each pair is finite and the second is non-finite:

1 The ship disappeared.
   The ship disappearing . . . .
2 Somebody speaks for a few minutes.
   Speaking for a few minutes . . . .
3 He mentioned the evidence.
   Mentioning the evidence . . . .
4 My landlady has been cooking cabbage.
   Having been cooking cabbage . . . .
5 He found the switch.
   To find the switch . . . .
6 The lake is choppy.
   For the lake to be choppy . . . .
7 The weather may be wet.
   For the weather to be wet . . . .

The key to the difference lies in an important distinction within the functioning of language. If you survey the list of examples given above, you

will see that the finite examples can function independently as communications with an addressee. We know that the person who utters a sentence like *The ship disappeared* is telling us something which he wishes us to regard as a fact. It is a declarative sentence. He could instead have spoken about the same subject-matter but have put it in the form that is technically known as **interrogative**: *Did the ship disappear?* In the latter case he would still be assuming that the idea of the ship disappearing had a truth value, but he would be appealing to the addressee to say what that truth value was: is it so or is it not so?

In contrast, the non-finite constructions do not distinguish between telling and asking; the speaker of an expression like *The ship disappearing . . .* is neither asserting that it is the case, nor requiring the addressee to say whether it is the case.

This, then, is the first point in the distinction between finite and non-finite constructions. And the form of the construction reflects the difference of function. Finite constructions have a subject and a verb, and it is the way these elements are arranged that indicates the speaker's communicative intention: *The ship disappeared* – subject before verb (declarative) – v. *Did the ship disappear?* – part of the verb phrase coming before the subject (interrogative). Non-finite constructions need not even have a subject and, if they do, there is certainly no possibility of changing its position to achieve a difference of communicative function.

A further point about finite constructions is that the speaker has the option of using modal verbs, thus introducing nuances of certainty, doubt, probability, and so on, into his communication. *The ship disappeared* is a straightforward declaration, but *The ship may have disappeared* is a statement merely of possibility. *The ship must have disappeared* expresses confidence, without claiming direct knowledge of the disappearance, only an inference. In contrast, non-finite constructions cannot possibly contain modal verbs.

Furthermore, finite constructions have tense; that is, the speaker has a choice between saying *The ship disappeared* and *The ship disappears*. If he chooses the first, the past tense, he means that the disappearance of the ship is somehow remote from the present occasion on which he is speaking – his claim will normally be understood as applying to some past occasion now over and done with. But, if he puts it in the present tense, he is speaking of the disappearance as part of the present state of the world. Non-finite constructions cannot distinguish the timing relative to the occasion of speaking; *the ship disappearing* is not timed – it is neither past nor present.

A last point needs to be made about finiteness. The relation between subject and verb in a finite construction is often marked by what is known as **agreement**, or **concord**, of the verb with the subject. For instance, in the present tense, a third person singular subject demands the use of the s-form of the first verb; all other subjects demand the base form. Thus we have *she sings*, and *the train goes by*, but *I sing*, *they sing*, *the trains go by*, etc.

There are certain considerations that limit the relevance of subject–verb agreement in English. Agreement is not realized with modal verbs as they have no s-form (e.g. *He mays arrive tomorrow*). Nor is agreement realized in the past tense: *she sang*, *I sang*, *the train went by*, *the trains went by*, etc. Here the verbs are *sang* and *went* whatever the subject; the d-form is used without any variation (see Figure 13, A, 3*a*, on p. 38). So it may look as though subject–verb agreement is not a very important principle in English grammar. It is certainly true that some languages, among them Spanish and Russian, have systems of agreement between subject and verb that are much more complicated and extensively manifested than the English system. But we still have to take account of the verb *be*. This verb is extremely common and for finite expressions it uses not three forms (base, s-form and d-form), but five: *am*, *are*, *is*, *was*, *were*. With this verb even the past tense has a

system for making the verb agree with the subject (Figure 13, A, 3*b*):

The train was going by
The trains were going by

Furthermore, there are extra forms (*am* and *are*, Figure 13, A, 1*b*) used in the present tense.

Finite constructions, by their very nature, can be independent of any verbal context. When they are uttered, we know how we are expected to react to what is being said without having to search around for an explanation. Non-finite constructions, on the other hand, do not have this independence. They are neither interrogative nor declarative, but are completely neutral to any such meaning. And they have no past or present tense; the contrast between past and present is just not possible. These facts are sufficient to account for the sense of incompleteness we get when we read:

The ship disappearing
With the ship disappearing
For the ship to disappear
Disappearing

In conclusion, we need to summarize the use of the terms finite and non-finite:

1   We can say of a verb phrase that it is finite or non-finite. If it is finite:
a   it has a subject;
b   there is a tense (past or present) associated with its first word (and the first word can be a modal auxiliary);
c   the first word is in agreement with the subject except under certain conditions described above.
If it is non-finite:
a   it need not have a subject;
b   it has no past or present tense, and cannot contain a modal auxiliary;
c   the first word is not in agreement with any subject.
2   The kind of construction which has a verb phrase and may have a subject and/or complements and adjuncts, is called a clause. (See

Chapter 5, p. 84, and glossary for further comments on the term **clause** as compared with **sentence**.) We may also use the terms finite and non-finite of clauses. If a clause contains a finite verb phrase, it is a finite clause; such clauses contain a subject. If a clause contains a verb phrase but has no finite verb phrase, then it is a non-finite clause.

(Exercises 8, 9 and 10 are on pp. 51–2.)

Verbs as complements

We saw on p. 37 that verbs can take a wide variety of expressions as their complements. Further study of the complementation of verbs will feature in Chapter 5. However, in order to provide a representative survey of the distribution of verbs, we now need to take note that verbs can themselves occur as the complements of verbs. For instance, the verb *want* can have either a noun phrase or a verb phrase as its complement:

> He wants a permit
> He wants to sleep

In the first of these, *a permit* is a noun phrase; in the second *to sleep* is a verb phrase. The verb *sleep* appears here with the word *to* in front of it. This word is called the **infinitive particle**. Expressions like *to sleep*, *to go*, *to see* are called infinitives, or to-infinitives. As the name suggests they are non-finite (see above, pp. 41–2), having no tense or subject agreement. Here are some further examples of sentences in which the main verb is complemented by a to-infinitive:

> The porter expects to find the key in the lock
> I am trying to close the door

In the first of these, the first verb phrase is *expects* and it is complemented by the infinitive *to find* which, in its turn, has a noun phrase as complement, *the key*. In the second example, the first verb phrase is *am trying*, with main verb *try*, and this is complemented by *to close* (which,

in its turn, has a noun phrase, *the door*, as complement).

We must be careful not to confuse to-infinitives with prepositional phrases beginning with the preposition *to* (see Chapter 2, p. 21):

> to London
> to the coast
> (he alluded) to their injuries

In these expressions *to* is followed by a noun phrase, not a verb phrase.

Sometimes a verb is complemented not by a to-infinitive but by some other non-finite form, usually by an ing-form:

> The house wants painting
> He continued singing

(Exercises 11 and 12 are on p. 52.)

Split infinitives

To-infinitives such as *to go*, *to catch*, *to see*, etc. are the 'infinitives' that people mean when they talk of split infinitives. **Split infinitives** are usually frowned upon by those who mention them. A sentence like *He wants to actually see them leave* is said to contain a split infinitive because the word *to* is separated from the word *see*. The descriptive linguist is concerned with what splittings of infinitives actually occur in the usage of English speakers. The usage is systematic and, as such, can be studied and described. For instance, only certain constructions are observed to occur. Nobody attests the occurrence of an expression like **He expects to the train meet*, instead of *He expects to meet the train*. But expressions like *He expects to suddenly see them* do occur; that is, there is a certain predictability about them. Upon reflection, of course, we realize that if this kind of expression did not have a systematic existence in the English language, there could not be any tradition about split infinitives being a 'bad thing'. If they occurred only randomly, as a result of 'crossed wiring' in the execution of speakers' plans – like **spoonerisms** – nobody would have anything to say against them, because it would be obvious that they were accidental. In the study of the sociology of language, however, it is interesting that the 'anti-split-infinitive' tradition exists; it is part of the social distribution of beliefs about the language.

Ing-forms and n-forms as modifiers

In Chapter 2 we saw that a noun phrase can have modifiers coming before the head. For instance, in the noun phrase *an angry dog*, *dog* is the head and *an* and *angry* are modifiers of the head. The word *angry* is an adjective (see Chapter 4 on adjectives). When adjectives are used to modify heads in a noun phrase, they normally come after any determiner and before the head. A similar kind of modification of the head can be achieved by the use of the ing-forms and n-forms of verbs. Thus the noun phrase *a barking dog* has *barking* as a modifier of the head *dog*. Here are some further examples:

a convincing victory
the crumbling walls
some moving targets
the waiting crowd
a coughing child
a satisfied customer
the relieved garrison
an interrupted session
a vanished ship

Pages 59–62 of Chapter 4 deal at more length with this use of ing-forms and n-forms.

Ing-forms as heads

The ing-forms of verbs can also be converted to a kind of noun-like use. Here are some examples of what we must regard as noun phrases since they have the definite article coming before a head and a prepositional phrase as post-modifier:

the breaking of the window
the burning of the toast
the examining of candidates by an
    external examiner

This construction is systematically related to various sentence patterns:

X breaks the window
The window breaks
The toast burns
The external examiner examines the
    candidates

(See Chapter 5, pp. 71–2, for a description of the sentence patterns; see glossary for **systematically related**.)

The ing-form of verbs can also have a noun-like function without any *of*-expression following. In the following sentences we can see from the use of the determiners that the ing-forms are, in essence, nouns:

All walking is good exercise
Some driving is enjoyable and
    recreational

Such words as *walking* and *driving* in the above are equivalent to uncountable nouns, and thus they can be used without any determiner:

Walking is good exercise
Driving is enjoyable and recreational

Voice and the verb

In the treatment of verb phrases, no mention has yet been made of the **passive voice**. The category of **voice** has two terms: **active** and **passive**. The verb phrases *eats* and *to eat* are active, while *is eaten* and *to be eaten* are passive:

The cat eats fish
(We expect) the cat to eat fish
Fish is eaten by the cat
(We expect) fish to be eaten by the cat

It can be seen that the contrast active v. passive is valid for both finite and non-finite verb phrases. In the passive voice the verb *be* is used as an auxiliary and this is followed by the n-form of the main verb (or the **past participle**). In the following examples the passive auxiliary is in italics:

is followed
am persecuted
will *be* eaten
may have *been* told
is *being* hidden
to have *been* broken

The significance of the distinction between active and passive is dealt with in Chapter 5 (see pp. 81–3).

Phrasal verbs

It is very frequent for a verb to be followed immediately or interruptedly by an element called an **adverbial particle**. The adverbial particles are minor-class words, many of which can also function as prepositions: *up*, *down*, *over*, *to*, *through*, *by*, etc. Here are some examples of sentences containing a verb followed by an adverbial particle:

They have *turned down* my application
They have *turned* my application *down*
I *looked up* their address
I *looked* their address *up*
He *read over* the first chapter
He *read* the first chapter *over*
We *separate out* the best candidates
We *separate* the best candidates *out*

The expressions *turn down*, *look up*, *read over*, and *separate out*, are called **phrasal verbs**. In all of the sentences just cited the phrasal verb has a complement in the form of a noun phrase: e.g. *my application*, *their address*, etc. This complement can come after the adverbial particle or between the verb and the adverbial particle. It is also possible to have a phrasal verb without a complement:

He is standing by
The papers are going through
They may turn back
Somebody has turned round already

There is sometimes a very striking difference between the use of a word like *down* as a preposition and as an adverbial particle:

He ran *down* the road (preposition)
He ran *down* the dog (adverbial particle)
He turned *up* the hill (preposition)
He turned *up* the heat (adverbial particle)

Prepositional verbs

There is another kind of construction very similar to phrasal verbs which, however, involves a verb followed by a prepositional phrase. Here are some examples:

He met with a rebuff
Their income depends on the business
I won't agree to his proposals
The occupants are participating in a witch-hunt

If the reader tests these sentences for the phrasal verb construction, he will find that they fail the test: the noun phrase cannot be switched with the preposition to give **he met a rebuff with*, etc. Nevertheless, the preposition depends closely on the verb; *meet* requires *with*, not *at*; *depend* requires *on*; *agree* requires *to*; etc. Linguists differ as to whether the complement in these constructions should be considered to be *with a rebuff* or simply *a rebuff*, but this is a matter that need not detain us at present. (Exercises 13, 14 and 15 are on p. 52.)

The meaning of verbs

So far in this chapter we have paid a great deal of detailed attention to criteria for identifying a class of words called verbs, and we have done this without referring at all to the kind of denotational meaning that these words have. We will now look at the meanings of verbs.

Words like *eat* denote **situations** in which people and things are related to each other. *Eat* refers to a situation involving two **participants** – an eater and a thing eaten. (It should be noted that the term *participant*, in this technical sense, refers not only to animate beings, but to inanimate objects as well.) Figure 15 is a diagram representing a situation in which John is the eater and a pie is the thing eaten. Whereas *John* and *the pie* are expressions that refer to two separate things, *eat* provides the connection between them in a particular situation. Verbs denote the relationship of participants to the situation in which they are playing a part.

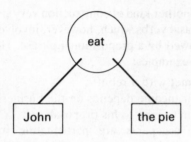

Figure 15

Two-place verbs

Eat is a verb that relates two participants; we can say that it is a **two-place verb**. Here are some other two-place verbs together with possible participants in the situation:

> tell (the witness, a lie)
> write (my solicitor, a letter)
> bring (the paperboy, today's *Guardian*)
> know (Bill, French)
> build (the Pharaohs, the pyramids)

It will be noticed that the kinds of situations that these verbs denote are extremely miscellaneous; eating is a very different kind of process from knowing, and both of these are very different from building. What they have in common is their relational sense; Bill and French are related by virtue of the fact that one of them knows the other, and the Pharaohs and the pyramids are related by virtue of the fact that the former built the latter.

It will also be observed that this type of verb meaning is entirely independent of such things as finiteness and tense. Thus 'know (Bill, French)' is a formula that will apply equally well to all of the following:

Bill knows French.
Does Bill know French?
Bill knew French.
Bill may know French.
Bill will know French.
. . . for Bill to know French . . .
. . . with Bill knowing French . . .
. . . knowing French, (Bill . . .)

Three-place verbs

In addition to two-place verbs there are **three-place verbs**, which denote a situation connecting three participants:

> give (Bill, my teacher, a houseplant) (*e.g.* Bill gave my teacher a houseplant: *or* Bill gave a houseplant to my teacher)
> tell (the children, their parents, an incredible story)
> grant (the authorities, him, permission to leave)
> put (the milkman, three bottles, the step) (*i.e.* The milkman put three bottles on the step)
> convert (the builders, the back room, a study) (*i.e.* The builders have converted the back room into a study)

Each verb determines the way the participants are arranged in the clause; for instance, *give* has the giver as subject and the recipient and the thing given as complements. The complements can be arranged either as (*Bill gave*) *my teacher a houseplant*, or as (*Bill gave*) *a houseplant to my teacher*. The verb *present*, although it is very similar in meaning to *give*, has different requirements: *Bill presented a houseplant to my teacher*, or *Bill presented my teacher with a houseplant*. Each verb has its own peculiar **syntax** – its power of determining the construction in which it occurs.

Some verbs allow a small range of alternative constructions, and other verbs do not. Thus, *present* varies between the two constructions just mentioned. A verb sometimes has a range of different senses, each sense determining a different construction. Thus *consider* occurs in both *He considered the problem* (He thought about it) and *He considered John foolish* (He judged him to be foolish).

One-place verbs

There are are also verbs that have only one participant. An example occurs in *The dog sleeps*. These are **one-place verbs**:

> sleep (the dog)
> shake (the house)
> fall (the leaves)
> ache (my finger)
> walk (I)

Even here we can see that the verbs denote a wide range of types of situation. Falling is a different kind of process from walking, since falling is something that happens to the faller, while walking is something that the walker does of his own volition. Despite this variety, the criterial meaning of the word-class 'verb' is present in all the words listed; *I* and *the leaves* denote participants in the situations and *fall* and *walk* denote the relation of the participants to the situation.

Intensive verbs

There is a particular class of verbs, sometimes known as **intensive** verbs, for which the concept of the verb as relater of participants is less apt. In a sentence like *The dog is friendly*, *the dog* is certainly a participant in a situation, but the same is not true of *friendly*. It seems more apt to view *be friendly* in its entirety as a kind of one-place 'verb', although it is made up of the verb *be* plus an **adjective phrase** (see the **predicative** function of **adjectives** in Chapter 4, p. 54). The same view could be taken of sentences like *The dog is a good companion* where *be a good companion* is made up of *be* plus a noun phrase. It seems unsatisfactory to view *the dog* and *a good companion* as distinct participants in a situation of 'being'; the complement in this case denotes a

characterization of the subject, not a separate participant.

The most common verb that has the property of linking a participant (the subject) with a characterizing complement is *be*. But other verbs are also employed, such as those in italics in the following sentences:

> The dog *appears* friendly
> The leaves *turned* brown
> The wind *became* a hurricane
> The farmyard *looks* dirty

More will be said about the syntax of these sentences in Chapter 5 (see pp. 72–4). (Exercise 16 is on p. 52.)

Dynamic and stative verbs

There is a difference between verbs that denote a **dynamic** situation – something that happens – and those that denote a static situation – a state of affairs that exists. *You ruined the concert* is dynamic. Sentences with dynamic verbs can be paraphrased with the expression *What happened was/is that . . .* ; e.g. *What happened was that you ruined the concert*. *Bill knew French* is not dynamic. It is **stative**, since we cannot gloss it by saying **What happened was that Bill knew French*. The verb *be* is most frequently used in a stative sense: *John was hungry* describes a state of affairs. The dynamic counterpart to this proposition is *John became hungry*. The verb *become* refers to a change in a state of affairs; processes of change are dynamic. The majority of verbs are dynamic in meaning. There are few stative verbs, though some of them, especially *be*, are of very frequent occurrence. (Exercise 17 is on p. 53.)

Derived verbs

The last part of our treatment of verbs has to do with the lexicon. Many verbs, like many nouns, are simple in their form; *eat* is structurally simple. In contrast, *frighten* is not simple; it can be broken down into *fright-* and *-en*. *Fright-* is the stem, and -*en* is a suffix. The stem by itself is not a verb but a noun (*I got a fright*). The effect of adding the suffix -*en* is to convert the noun into a verb. So the presence of this suffix is a clue to the fact that the word in which it occurs is a verb.

Here are further examples of verbs that are 'derived' from other words: *activate* (from *active*), *symbolize* (from *symbol*), *whiten* (from *white*), *purify* (from *pure*), *materialize* (from *material*), *falsify* (from *false*), *deepen* (from *deep*), *equalize* (from *equal*), *criticize* (from *critic*), *differentiate* (from *different*), *quicken* (from *quick*). The suffixes exemplified in these words are: -*ate*, -*ize*, -*ify*, -*en*. (Exercise 18 is on p. 53.)

The suffixes -*ate*, -*ize*, -*ify*, -*en*, can often be recognized as forming part of a verb even when the stem to which they are added is not an independently existing word. For instance, *calculate* is a verb but there is no independent word **calcul*. The analysis into *calcul-* and -*ate* is, however, supported by reference to the word *calculus*. Other words where the termination is recognizable as the verb-forming suffix -*ate* are: *initiate*, *dominate* and *isolate*. This termination is therefore a fairly reliable signal that the word in question is a verb. The same is true of the other verb-forming suffixes, as these words demonstrate: *recognize*, *magnify*, *rectify*. (Exercise 19 is on p. 53.)

A few verbs in English are formed with a prefix; *belittle* and *befriend* both have the prefix *be-*, and *enslave* has the prefix *en-*. These are far less numerous than the verbs formed with the suffixes described above.

There are a very large number of words in English that can be used as either nouns or verbs without any change of form. We can say *The auctioneer will value the picture*, and *The picture has a high value*. In the first sentence *value* is a verb, and in the second it is a noun. Thus the word can be sometimes one and sometimes the other, and we cannot tell which unless we look at the context. (Exercise 20 is on p. 53.)

Of some words that can be used both as nouns and as verbs, it is possible to say that they are first and foremost nouns and that their use as verbs is secondary, or derived. The word *chair* is basically a noun, and in *He chaired the meeting* the verb *to chair* is derived from the noun. Conversely, some words are basically verbs and their use as nouns is derived. *Drive* is a verb, and the noun meaning 'an approach to a house along which one drives' is derived from the verb. On the other hand, there are scores of words that seem more or less equally balanced between being a verb and a noun, and it would be difficult to judge whether one use was primary and the other derived. Among these are *slope*, *cover*, *mind*, *name*, *step* and *change*. (Exercise 21 is on p. 53.)

A further interesting point about the **conversion** of nouns to verbs and vice versa is that some words are merely pronounced differently according to whether they are nouns or verbs; there is no additional suffix, and there is sometimes not even any difference in the way the word is written down in ordinary spelling. The word *house* has an /s/ sound when it is a noun (it rhymes with *mouse*), but has a /z/ sound (to rhyme with *rouse*) when it is a verb. Other words that are like this are *use*, *grieve/grief*, and *strive/strife*, though the different spelling of the last two records the difference in sound.

The words *conduct*, *import*, *present* and *insult* can be both nouns and verbs. The words are written without any change of spelling, but the reader who is familiar with the pronunciation of English will recognize that the **stress** is placed on the first syllable if it is a noun and on the second syllable if it is a verb: ínsult (n.), insúlt (v.). The following sentences illustrate this:

His cónduct was disgraceful
The wires condúct the electric current
The country's ímports include coal
The country impórts coal
I have given him a présent
I shall presént him with a book
What an ínsult!
They insúlt us

On the other hand, there are words that seem to be constructed on a similar pattern but which do not shift the stress: *réscue* has the stress on the first syllable whether it is a noun or a verb, and *disgráce* normally has the stress on the second syllable. (Exercise 22 is on p. 53.)

The word *dispute* is of some interest since one nowadays often hears people pronounce the noun with the stress on the first syllable: *The díspute has lasted three weeks*. The older pronunciation, on the other hand, has the stress on the second syllable. It seems that there is a tendency for people to treat this word like *conduct*, *insult*, etc. and to make the stress variable. However, speakers are divided on this point, so it must be regarded as an unstable feature of present-day English. (It is possible to describe such a state of affairs in contemporary English usage without disparaging the people who have adopted the new pronunciation, and without making out that their language is anarchic. It is clear that the new usage, though different from the old, is no less systematic. See Chapter 1, pp. 13–14.) (Exercise 23 is on p. 53.)

Verbs converted from adjectives

There are a certain number of words that are primarily adjectives but which can also be used as verbs. For example, *busy* is primarily an adjective, and its use in the sentence *The assistant is rather busy* is typical. Adjectives form the subject-matter of the next chapter, so we are to some extent anticipating that discussion. What we need to observe here is that the word *busy* can also be used, without any modification of form, as a verb:

> The assistant is busying himself with the accounts

Some other adjectives that are converted to use as verbs are shown in the following examples. The words in question are printed in italics.

> The car is *slow*ing down
> Putting the pan on the window sill will help to *cool* it

> He *pale*d at the thought

As with the conversion of verbs to nouns and nouns to verbs, there are some words capable of being used either way without it being possible to say which use is primary. The word *clean* is a verb in *He is cleaning the window*, but an adjective in *The window is clean*.

Exercises

Exercise 1

Using the method of combining words with *I, you, he, she, it, we, they*, decide whether the following words are verbs or not. (You should add an '-s' suffix when the pronoun you choose is *he, she* or *it*.)

> Caravan, listen, suppose, leave, stand, blink, heartily, biscuit, room, creak, Paris, scatter, turmoil, comic, promise, intrusive, sombre, none, child

Exercise 2

Which of these expressions are instances of the subject–verb construction and which are not? For those that are, are they in the present tense or the past tense?

> a new situation develops
> after a last-minute rush
> fourteen skilled forestry workers
> agricultural shows in the area
> a well-known local farmer died
> the lights shine
> everybody left
> very valuable indeed

Exercise 3

There are quite a number of verbs in the following passage. Pick out the combinations of subject + verb and list them. Underline the verb or the subject in order to make it quite clear which is which. (For example, from lines one and two: *he* swayed; *he* walked; *the camel at the zoo* sways. Subjects in italics.)

He swayed slightly as he walked, as the camel at the zoo sways from side to side when it walks along the asphalt path laden with grocers and their wives. . . . The camel despises the grocers; the camel is dissatisfied with its lot; the camel sees the blue lake and the fringe of palm trees in front of it. So the great jeweller, the greatest jeweller in the whole world, swung down Piccadilly, perfectly dressed, with his gloves, with his cane; but dissatisfied still, till he reached . . . the dark little shop in the street off Bond Street.

As usual, he strode through the shop window without speaking, though the four men . . . stood straight and looked at him. . . .

(Virginia Woolf, *The Duchess and the Jeweller*)

Exercise 4

Consider the inflectional paradigm of each of the verbs identified in Exercise 3. Make out two tables of forms like Figure 14, with five columns each, one column for each form. Let one table be for regular verbs and the other for irregular verbs. (Omit the word *is* from consideration for the time being; we shall be coming to it soon.)

Exercise 5

The following passage formed part of a speech made to the Oxford Union in December 1958, by the humorist Gerard Hoffnung. For a time it became a very well-known anecdote.

A striking lesson in keeping the upper lip stiff is given in a recent number of the *Weekly Bulletin* of the Federation of Civil Engineering Contractors, which prints the following letter from a
5   bricklayer in Golders Green to the firm for whom he worked:

'Respected Sir,
. . . When I got to the top of the building, I found that the hurricane had knocked some bricks off
10   the top. So I rigged up a beam with a pulley at the top of the building and hoisted up a couple of barrels of bricks. When I had fixed the building there was† a lot of bricks left over. I hoisted the barrel back up again and secured the line at the
15   bottom, and then went up and filled the barrel with extra bricks. Then I went to the bottom and cast off the line.
Unfortunately, the barrel of bricks was heavier than I was, and before I knew what was
20   happening, the barrel started down, jerking me off the ground.
I decided to hang on, and half way up I met the barrel coming down, and received a severe blow on the shoulder. I then continued to the top,
25   banging my head against the beam and getting my fingers jammed in the pulley.
When the barrel hit the ground, it bursted† its bottom allowing all the bricks to spill out. I was now heavier than the barrel, and so started down
30   again at high speed.
Half way down I met the barrel coming up and received a severe injury to my shins. When I hit the ground, I landed on the bricks, getting several painful cuts from the sharp edges.
35   At this point I must have lost my presence of mind, because I let go the line. The barrel then came down, giving me another heavy blow on the head and putting me in hospital.

I respectfully request sick leave.'

(† The bricklayer from Golders Green had some non-standard features in his English.)

1   Take lines 7–17 of the passage and make a list of the subject + verb combinations. Underline the verb (in two cases it is a phrase of two verbs); e.g. for line 8: I *got*; I *found*. There are seven such combinations altogether. There are five more verbs that do not occur immediately with their subject because the subject has been left out: e.g. in line 11 . . . *and hoisted* . . . means '. . . and I hoisted . . .', where *I* is the subject. This is an instance of ellipsis of the subject. (NB   Ignore the occurrence of the words *there was*. This construction will be given attention later, see p. 74.)

2   Pick out all the verbs you can find in lines 18–39. (NB   The forms of *be – is* and *was* – should be omitted; so should *must*.) For each verb

a state which form it is in;
b state whether the verb is regular or irregular;

c state the base form;

d if the verb is irregular, add it to the table of forms you started for irregular verbs in Exercise 4.

(If the same form comes up a second time do not include it again.)

Exercise 6

1 Using the verb *give*, fill in the missing expressions from the following table:

1a	present	give
	present perfect	. . . . .
	present perfect continuous	have been giving
1b	present continuous	. . . . .
		am giving
2	present	. . . . .
	present perfect	has given
	present perfect continuous	. . . . .
	present continuous	. . . . .
3a	past	. . . . .
	past perfect	. . . . .
	past perfect continuous	had been giving
3b	past continuous	. . . . .
		. . . . .

2 What labels (e.g. past perfect, etc.) should be attached to these forms?

a has trodden; *b* fell; *c* were driving; *d* have been showing; *e* had been showing.

Exercise 7

Fill in the forms missing from this table. The section numbers correspond to those in Figure 13 (p. 38), i.e. 1–2 for the present tense and 3 for the past tense:

1–2	modal present	may grow
	modal present perfect	may have grown
	modal present perfect continuous	. . . . .
	modal present continuous	. . . . .
3	modal past	might grow
	modal past perfect	. . . . .
	modal past perfect continuous	might have been growing
	modal past continuous	. . . . .

Exercise 8

1 In the following clauses underline the verb phrase. Which of them are finite and which are non-finite? (Punctuation and capital letters are omitted so that these do not give you any clue to the answers.)

> the caretaker found the soap under the sink
> have you seen my scarf
> the building being newly built
> for Jack to arrive in time
> we are asking you soon
> having tried to contact you
> his sister may be flying home
> was his sister flying home
> his sister having been flying home

2 For those that are finite, what is the tense (look at the first word)? Change the tense from present to past or vice versa.

Exercise 9

Turn to the passage quoted for Exercise 5 (p. 50) and list all the non-finite clauses. (There are several that begin with an ing-form.) None of them have a subject, but if you examine the context you should be able to write a corresponding finite clause with a subject. Thus, the first non-finite clause is *jerking me off the ground* (lines 20–1). The corresponding finite clause would be *The barrel jerked me off the ground*, which has *the barrel* as subject.

Exercise 10

To assess the importance of subject–verb agreement in English do an analysis of a piece of text. Take a few paragraphs of a newspaper article and pick out the finite verbs. What proportion of the finite verbs realize agreement between verb and subject? i.e. how many could appear in a different form if the subject were changed in person and number?

Exercise 11

Look at the passage quoted in Exercise 27 of Chapter 2 (p. 35) and find any instances of to-infinitives. Also note any instances of *to* as a preposition.

Exercise 12

Write sentences in which the following verbs are complemented by other verbs. Note whether the complement is an infinitive or an ing-form.

> keep, try, begin, finish, manage, like,
> mean, pretend, agree

Exercise 13

Look at these sentences and find examples of phrasal verbs, i.e. of verbs followed by adverbial particles. Ignore any prepositional constructions.

> I have made up a bed for you
> They turned out in large numbers
> He is coming down tomorrow
> He is coming down the road
> Her little girl pointed to some toys

Exercise 14

Search the passage quoted in Exercise 5 (p. 50) for instances of phrasal verbs with or without a complement.

Exercise 15

Take the verbs *put*, *wash*, *write*, *hear*, *light* and *split*, and write sentences in which they occur together with adverbial particles.

Exercise 16

1 Analyse these sentences from the point of view of the type of situation they refer to:
  a identify the verb (sometimes with a preposition dependent on it);
  b identify the participants;
  c if there is only one participant and it has an attribute, say what the attribute is.

  i   He approached the Ministry of Agriculture
  ii   The Ministry gave him a substantial grant
  iii The Council negotiates with the occupier
  iv   The farmer is a trustee
  v   They will make a fundamental change
  vi   They weigh the public interest against the private
  vii This involves a growth of bureaucracy
  viii Such people appear powerless
  ix   The public interest suffered

2 Think of some short sentences containing the following verbs and for each sentence decide what the participants in the situation are. (NB Some sentences contain circumstantial elements besides the verb and the participants. For instance, *The children told their parents an incredible story last night* has not only three participants: *the children*, *their parents*, and *an incredible story*; but it also has some circumstantial detail – the timing of the happening: *last night*. In your answers you can include as much circumstantial detail as you like.)

The verbs for you to work on are:

> lend, launch, attach, combine, speak,
> utter, write, drive, break, sleep

(Remember that many verbs can be used in more ways than one. *Move* occurs both in *The curtain moved* and in *Somebody moved the curtain*. This is quite apart from the other sense of the verb found in *The experience moved her to tears*.)

Exercise 17

Which of the following contain dynamic verbs and which stative?

Jack went up the hill
Mary sold Henry her old Ford
Henry owned the old Ford
The old Ford is in the garage
Jack is hungry
Jack is getting hungry
The old Ford still seems serviceable
The accident happened yesterday
The objection stands
Bill slams the door
That building looks modern
Mary seems disappointed
My next-door neighbour is the Lord Mayor

Exercise 18

What are the words that the following verbs are derived from? Are any of them nouns?

diversify, particularize, disagree, signify, soften, endanger, symbolize

Exercise 19

Find six to ten verbs that end in the suffix *-ize*. For each one note whether the stem to which it is attached is a word or not. For instance, *recognize* has the suffix *-ize*, but **recogn* is not an independently existing word. On the other hand, *tenderize* has the same suffix and *tender* is also a word.

Exercise 20

Decide whether the word in italics is a verb or a noun and then write another sentence in which it is used in the other way. For instance, in the first example, *ship* is a verb, and in the sentence *The ship came into harbour this morning, ship* is a noun.

We are going to *ship* the cargo next week
He will probably *phrase* his letter carefully
This *exercise* is not too difficult
Will you put these papers in the *file*, please?
The chef *cooks* twenty turkeys a day
I have cut three *branches* from the apple tree
I am trying to have a nice *sleep*
They want a *say* in the running of the *place*
He *commands* them to stay at their *posts*
The housekeeper will line the drawer with *paper*

Exercise 21

Compose two sentences for each of the following words, one in which it is used as a verb and the other in which it is used as a noun:

slope, cover, mind, name, step, change

Exercise 22

For each of the following words, investigate whether the stress is constant or shifting. If you are doubtful about them, compose some sentences and ask your friends to read them aloud (without telling them what you are interested in).

discount, disguise, dismay, disgust, dislike, disgrace, dispute, discharge

Exercise 23

Which of the following words have a change in stress according to whether they are used as a noun or as a verb?

object, progress, project, display, mistake, repair, reject, research, concern, conflict, decoy

4 Adjectives and adjective phrases

The predicative function

The typical **adjective** is able to function as a complement after the verb *be*. The following examples have the adjectives underlined.

> The festival is *lively*
> His voice was *harsh*
> This problem has been *difficult*
> No man is *infallible*
> Your behaviour was *foolhardy*
> The music is *loud*
> The materials in use are *brittle*
> Those potatoes were *hot*

When an adjective occurs in this position it is said to be **predicated** of the subject: *lively* is predicated of *the festival*, *brittle* is predicated of *the materials in use*, and so on. This function of adjectives is therefore said to be the **predicative** function.

It is not only adjectives that can be predicated of a subject. Nouns also can be used in this way, as in *The festival is an expense*, *This problem has been the stumbling block* and *The men are students*. So how can we tell the difference between an adjective and a noun? It is partly a question of what happens when an adjective phrase contains more than a head. The words that can act as modifier to an adjective head are different from those that can act as modifier to a noun head:

> His voice was very harsh

This problem has been somewhat difficult
The potatoes were terribly hot
Some tigers are quite docile

The words acting as modifiers to the adjective heads in these examples are *very*, *somewhat*, *terribly* and *quite*. The name for this kind of modifier in adjective phrases is **intensifier**. In noun phrases the noun head may have a determiner, while adjective heads cannot have determiners. We can say *every chair* but not **every hot*; and we can say *terribly hot* but not **terribly chair*. Figure 16 shows the structure of the adjective phrase.

intensifier	head
very	harsh
somewhat	difficult
terribly	hot

Figure 16

Furthermore, nouns can be inflected for plural number – at least, countable nouns can – while adjectives cannot. **The men were hungries* is not a possible sentence, while *The men were students* is all right.

It is not only the verb *be* that can take an adjective phrase as its complement. There are some other verbs that can do so:

The festival seems very lively
His voice sounded harsh
This problem has proved quite difficult
Your behaviour appeared foolhardy
The materials in use became rather brittle
The potatoes got terribly hot
Your little girl looks pale

This list of examples has the verbs *seem*, *sound*, *prove*, *appear*, *become*, *get* and *look*. (Exercises 1 and 2 are on p. 67.)

The attributive function

We have seen that adjectives can be used in predicative function. They can also function as modifiers of nouns in noun phrases. This fact was pointed out in Chapter 2, when we were dealing with the ways to identify nouns (see p. 20 above). Here are some examples of noun phrases with adjectives acting as modifiers in front of the head (the adjectives are in italics):

> the *lively* festival
> his *harsh* voice
> this *difficult* problem
> *infallible* men
> *foolhardy* behaviour
> some *loud* music
> the *brittle* materials
> three *hot* potatoes

Adjectives that act as modifiers of noun heads are said to have an **attributive** function.

In general, when an adjective can be predicated of a subject, it also makes sense to use that same adjective as a modifier of the subject noun: *The festival is lively* thus has a systematic relation to *the lively festival*, and so on.

Whether an adjective is appearing in attributive or predicative function, it can equally well have an intensifier like *very* or *extremely* coming in front of it:

> A very lively festival –
> The festival is very lively

> Extremely pleasing results –
> The results are extremely pleasing

Some pretty awful programmes –
The programmes are pretty awful
Highly confidential information –
The information is highly confidential
An amazingly powerful engine –
The engine is amazingly powerful

Here we can see that what acts as a modifier to the head of a noun phrase is not just a single adjective but an **adjective phrase**. Figure 17 shows the structure.

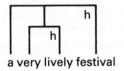

Figure 17

In this construction there are two heads; *lively* is the head of the adjective phrase *very lively*, and *festival* is the head of the noun phrase *a very lively festival*.

The great majority of adjectives can occur both predicatively and attributively. There are, however, some that are more restricted in their occurrence. For example, *the chief reason* is not systematically related to a predication: **the reason is chief*. We shall be looking at these again later (see p. 65).

Inflection of adjectives

There are very many adjectives that have a paradigm of inflected forms such as the following:

> large, larger, largest
> bright, brighter, brightest

The first item in these lists is uninflected, the second, which has the suffix *-er*, is said to be inflected for **comparative degree**, and the last, with the suffix *-est*, is inflected for **superlative degree**. There are a few adjectives that have irregular inflected forms:

> bad, worse, worst
> good, better, best

More important, however, is the fact that many adjectives do not have comparative and superlative inflections at all. For instance, there are no forms *dociler* and *docilest*, or *difficulter*, and *difficultest*. (Exercises 3 and 4 are on p. 67.)

The adjectives above, which do not have inflected forms, *stylisher*, *regularest*, etc., certainly do not lack inflections because they cannot reflect the concepts of comparative and superlative degree. After all, *hard* and *difficult* have much the same meaning in *This work is hard* and *This work is difficult*, and yet only the first can be changed to *This work is harder*. For the second, we use a phrasal expression of comparative degree: *This work is more difficult*. Similarly we have *This work is the most difficult*, not *This work is the difficultest*.

The fact that words such as *difficult* cannot take inflections, therefore, is not due to their meaning. It is more a question of their structure. The adjectives that can be inflected are usually those that are simple in structure (i.e. those that do not contain prefixes or suffixes), and this means, of course, that almost all monosyllabic adjectives can be inflected: *small*, *bright*, *harsh*, etc. There are also two-syllable adjectives included among them: *clever*, *narrow*, *polite* and so on. Adjectives that are derived from other words by the addition of suffixes like *-ish*, *-ful*, *-al*, *-able*, *-ar*, etc., tend not to take the inflections. However, this is only a tendency; the suffixes *-y* and *-ly*, in *cloudy* and *friendly*, do not preclude the use of *-er* and *-est*: *cloudier*, *friendlier*, *funniest*, and *homeliest*.

Gradability

If something is 'hot', it may be 'not very hot' or 'intensely hot' or somewhere in between; there is an open-ended, continuous scale of 'hotness'. Adjectives that express this kind of meaning are called **gradable** adjectives.

Not all adjectives are gradable; or perhaps it would be more accurate to say that adjectives are not always intended to be interpreted in a gradable sense. The ordinary interpretation of the word *tubular* in the expression *tubular bells*, or of *poetic* in *poetic licence* is not that it denotes a gradable quality, but that it denotes a type or category of bells or licence. Licence is either of the poetic type or it is not, it cannot be 'fairly poetic'. Similarly bells cannot be 'amazingly tubular'. Passing over this other kind of adjective for the present, let us examine the notion of gradability in more detail.

If an adjective is gradable, it makes sense to ask 'How?'; *how hot?*, *how attractive?*, etc. That is to say, we can ask for a gradation of the quality referred to. If somebody is talking about some high-rise flats, we can ask, 'How tall are they?' The answer we receive might be one of several kinds. First of all, we could be given an explicit and precise measure: *twelve storeys*, *150 feet*, etc. (Quite often, of course, this kind of precise measure is not possible. There is no such exact way to answer the question *How hostile was your reception?* or *How attractive is the picture?*) As a second alternative, the degree of tallness might be stated with an intensifier: *very*, *quite*, or *moderately*. Third, it could be stated comparatively: *taller than the other buildings*; *less tall than you would expect*. Finally, it could be stated superlatively: *The tallest I have ever seen*, *The least tall in that part of the town*. Therefore, leaving aside the first kind of answer (*150 feet*), to which we shall here pay no further attention, there are three kinds of gradation: **intensifying**, **comparative** and **superlative**. The following description of gradability applies to both inflectable adjectives (e.g. *tall*, *taller*, *tallest*) and to non-inflectable ones (e.g. *imposing*, *more imposing*, *most imposing*).

Intensification

Gradability always implies a scale of comparison even when none of the three types of gradation is being used. A 'large' tree is large only by comparison with a norm for trees. Similarly, a tree can be considered small only if we have some conception of what size is ordinary for trees. The 'norm' that we refer to when assessing the degree of some quality depends, of course, on our cultural background: it is understood without necessarily being expressed.

There is another interesting thing about this kind of adjective. *Large* and *small* are 'opposites', but the kind of opposition between them is such that a tree may be neither large nor small, but middle-sized. *Not large* does not imply 'small', and *not small* does not imply 'large'. Pairs of words that are opposite in meaning in this way are said to be *antonyms*. Figure 18 suggests this kind of opposition.

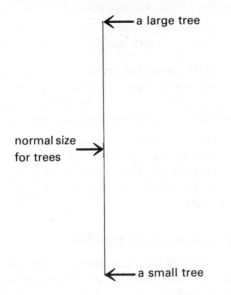

Figure 18

Many gradable adjectives go in pairs of antonyms like *large* and *small*. When one of these adjectives occurs in questions with *how*, it is neutral to any place on the scale. Thus, *How large is that tree?* does not presuppose that the tree is on the large side as trees go. The answer could be *It's quite small*, without any sense of contradiction. It is equivalent to asking *What size is that tree?* On the other hand, *how small is that tree?* does presuppose smallness by comparison with the norm. In this pair of antonyms, *large* is the 'neutral' term because it is the one

that is used when we do not wish to prejudge the issue. (Exercise 5 is on p. 67.)

The use of intensifiers to modify adjectives (as in *extremely large*, *quite large*, *fairly small*, etc.) has the effect of placing the graded object further from, or nearer to, the centre of the scale in Figure 18.

Comparison

Comparison does not refer to an implicit norm. Some other object is used for the purpose of comparison and the graded object is measured against it. Thus, *This tree is larger* can only be understood if we can answer the question *Larger than what?* The answer is not 'the norm for trees' but some other object, possibly, but not necessarily, another tree. The missing information may be given immediately after the comparative expression: *This tree is larger than the one in that field*. Or it may be discoverable only by back reference.

We must note that saying that a tree is larger than another tree, or larger than something that is not a tree, does not mean that it is a large tree; it could be quite small as trees in general go.

In general there are three types of comparison. We can say that something has more of a quality (the **superior** relation), or less of a quality (the **inferior** relation), or just as much of a quality (the **equal** relation):

> heavier/more interesting (than . . .)
>   (*superior*);
> less heavy/less interesting (than . . .)
>   (*inferior*);
> as heavy/as interesting (as . . .) (*equal*).

There is another kind of the 'equal' comparative relation. It is rather like the 'as . . . as' kind that we find in *This document is as long as that one*. But this time, instead of comparing the length of one document with that of another, we compare it with the length that would be required for some result to follow. *This document is so long that I haven't time to read it*; i.e. its length is greater than the maximum length that would allow me to have time to read it. The same meaning can be expressed with the words *too* and *enough* used as modifiers to the adjective:

> The mountain is so high that the top is in the clouds
>
> The mountain is high enough for the top to be in the clouds
>
> The mountain is so high that nobody has climbed it
>
> The mountain is too high for anybody to have climbed it

A curious thing about the word *enough* is that it comes after the adjectival head instead of before it, while *too* comes in the usual position: *too high*, but *high enough*. The part of the adjective phrase that comes after the head is quite complex in structure, and the structure varies in different types of expression. Beyond showing the overall principle of structure for such phrases (Figure 19) we shall not go into this matter further. The adjective phrases in Figure 19 have the adjective as the head and the other elements in the structure are pre-modifiers or post-modifiers.

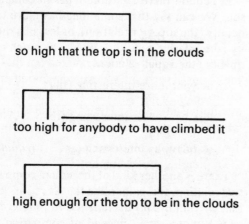

Figure 19

Superlatives

Superlative gradation also refers to an explicit standard rather than to a norm. But it places the graded object at the extreme end of the scale. For instance, *the largest tree* takes a whole range of trees as its field of reference, and we have to know what range is being referred to in order to understand the expression. If we ask *The largest in what range?* the information may be given immediately – *The largest tree in that wood* – or it may be given by back reference. The tree referred to is not, of course, necessarily large in comparison with the norm for trees in general.

Superlatives require the definite article when they are used attributively: *the longest film*. When they are used predicatively they usually have the article, but not always:

> This film is longest
> This film is the longest

Superlatives can take either a 'superior' or an 'inferior' form (*longest*, or *least long*). If one combines this choice with the choice between two antonyms, there are four forms of expression:

the longest film	the most precise answer
the shortest film	the vaguest answer
the least long film	the least precise answer
the least short film	the least vague answer

Non-gradable adjectives: colour

If we are told that somebody's tie is red, we might ask what shade of red it is, but it would scarcely make sense to ask *How red?* The tie might be *bright red*, or *dull red*, or *cherry red*, but not usually *rather red* or *extremely red*. These latter expressions are not totally meaningless, but if somebody says *extremely red* he is probably not thinking so much of the shade of colour but of the garish quality of the tie. In other words, if the word *red* is being used as a 'quality' adjective, it makes sense to say *very red*, or *the reddest I have ever seen*, etc., but if it is really being used as a colour adjective, the kind of **modification** we expect is not the grading type, but the type that tells us the shade of colour. So we need to make a distinction between adjectives that make a **qualitative** modification of the head, and adjectives that make a colour modification of the head. (Exercise 6 is on p. 67.)

Non-gradable adjectives: classifying

Here are two lists of noun phrases containing attributive adjectives. Those in the first list could not easily have any kind of gradability associated with them, while those in the second could.

1   the general election
    a deliberate liar
    these strategic weapons
    its charitable status
    private foundations like the Gulbenkian
    a musical version of the play
    a wild animal
    a black mamba

2   a bitter denunciation
    an unrealistic proposal
    this important work
    its wistful charm
    the reassuring reports
    a musical personality
    these heavy stones
    this wild region

The adjectives in list 1 cannot be treated as gradable: *very strategic weapons*; *This election is the most general we have met with*; *Foundations like the Gulbenkian are extremely private*. There is no kind of election that is midway between being general and local. Thus, it makes no sense to say *a very general election* unless by some feat of the imagination you can interpret the word general, in this context, as gradable.

Adjectives like those in list 1, above, are **classifying** adjectives; elections are classified, and *general* is one of the classes. The classifications denoted are largely institutional – legal, military, academic, etc. Quite often people invent systems of classification for special uses, and employ 'ordinary' gradable adjectives

for denoting these new classes. In a greengrocer's shop the potatoes are either new or old and each kind has its own price; you cannot have 'fairly new' ones. Thus the difference between gradable and ungradable adjectives is not altogether a matter of knowing the properties of isolated words; one has to take the **context** into account as well.

Noun phrases may contain several adjective modifiers. The patterns in which the adjectives occur when there is more than one can sometimes be fairly complex. We are not going to describe these patterns in much detail here. But it is of interest to note that the sequence: qualitative, colour, classifying, is the usual one as far as these three kinds are concerned:

> a large grey modern sculpture
> a charming tiled roof
> a small blue flower
> yellow oil-bound paint
> a strange granular texture

The reader should try changing the sequence of the adjectives in these phrases and see what curious expressions result: *a tiled charming roof*, etc. (Exercise 7 is on p. 67.)

Gradable ing-forms

In Chapter 3 (p. 44) it was pointed out that the ing-forms of verbs are often used as modifiers of nouns. To what extent are ing-forms like attributive adjectives? Here are some examples which will help us to answer this question:

1   a surprising coincidence
    a pleasing entertainment
    an exciting novel
    some disparaging remarks
    an insulting letter
    some damning evidence
    a flattering speech
    a shattering experience

2   a charging bull
    an opening window
    a crying child

a breaking wave
an ageing clergyman
a working arrangement
a protesting demonstrator

We will leave aside the examples in group 2 until later. The examples in group 1 contain ing-forms that are gradable like many of the adjectives we have been looking at. So we could have *a rather surprising coincidence*, *an extremely flattering speech*, *the most shattering experience of my life*, *How damning was the evidence?*, etc. These are qualitative modifiers of the head. It is also possible to use them predicatively just as though they were adjectives:

The coincidence is *surprising*
The entertainment was *quite pleasing*
The novel is *very interesting*
His letter was *pretty insulting*

We should notice that an expression like *was insulting*, taken out of context, is ambiguous. Put into a context, the difference between the two interpretations usually becomes plain:

His letter was insulting
The speaker was insulting his audience

In the first of these sentences *insulting* is a predicative ing-form and, since it is gradable, we could also say *His letter was very insulting*. But in the second sentence insulting is part of a verb phrase; *be insulting* is the continuous form of the verb *insult*, and it could be contrasted with other forms of the verb phrase like *insulted*, *had insulted*, *had been insulting*, *may have insulted*, etc.

Noun phrases such as *an exciting novel*, in which the head is modified by a qualitative ing-form, are systematically related to sentences of the type:

The novel excites one

In such sentences the subject (*the novel*) is possibly an inanimate entity, and the complement is somebody who is affected by the process referred to by the verb. The following sentences are all systematically related to noun phrases similar to *an exciting novel*:

The meal satisfies one
The experience humiliates one
The result astonishes one
The performance excites one
The journey tries one
The phrase chills one
The dream torments one
The medicine rejuvenates one

Non-gradable ing-forms

The examples listed in group 2 above (pp. 59–60), *a charging bull*, etc., are not qualitative modifiers since they are not gradable. We cannot say **a rather charging bull*; **This window is more opening than you would think*; **the most crying child in the world*; **The arrangement is so working that we shall change it next week*; **How breaking is the wave?* These are non-gradable modifiers and they obviously have something in common with classifiers.

They are also different from the gradable type in other interesting ways. For one thing, the sentences to which they are systematically related are of a rather different kind:

The bull charges
The window opens
The child cries
The wave breaks
The clergyman ages
The arrangement works

These sentences consist of a subject and a verb but have no complement; comparison with sentences like *The meal satisfies one* reveals several differences, but we shall not be in a position to describe these in detail until the next chapter (see pp. 71–2).

Furthermore, there is no possibility of these non-gradable ing-forms being used predicatively. If we change *a breaking wave* to the sentence *The wave is breaking*, we end up with just a subject–verb sentence; the subject is *the wave* and the verb is the continuous form of the verb *to break*. There is no way in which we could see *breaking* as a predicative adjective; for instance, we cannot have **The wave is very breaking*.

It follows from what has been said about ing-forms here and in Chapter 3, that an expression like *moving targets* is ambiguous. It could be a non-finite clause (as in *Moving targets is hard work*), or it could be a noun phrase with *targets* as the head and *moving* as a modifier (as in *Moving targets are difficult to hit*). (Exercises 8, 9 and 10 are on p. 68.)

A type of compound adjective

Before we leave ing-forms, it would be worth looking at another kind of modifier: *man-eating*, *spine-chilling*, *body-building*, etc. This kind is compounded out of two words, a noun and an ing-form. *Man-eating* is compounded out of *man* and *eating*; the noun *man* is understood as the complement of the verb *eat*, so that from *tiger eats man* we get *man-eating tiger*, and from *the tale chills the spine* we get *spine-chilling tale*. We might reasonably regard words like *spine-chilling* and *man-eating* as lexical items, rather than expressions produced at need (see the discussion on **productivity** in Chapter 2, pp. 27–8). And it is true that these words are to be found in dictionaries. But it seems that they are also coinable by rule. In an autobiography I found the expression *my peace-destroying note*, though I doubt if there is any dictionary that records the word *peace-destroying*. Similarly, we could coin expressions like a *novel-reading passenger*, *tax-evading employee*, *power-seizing general*, etc.

A type of compound noun

At this point we need to take care not to confuse attributive ing-forms, which are adjectival in character, with ing-forms that are essentially noun-like. In Chapter 3 (p. 44) we saw that ing-forms can be used as uncountable nouns in such sentences as *All walking is good exercise*, and *Driving is enjoyable*. We also find ing-forms

of a noun-like character being used to form compound words such as: *working-party*, *driving-offences*, *swimming-pool*, *eating apples*, *speaking-tube*, *waiting-room*, *performing rights* and *firing-squad*. These can be explained as 'party for working', 'offences concerning driving', 'pool for swimming', 'apples for eating', etc., in which the ing-forms are uncountable nouns. The use of hyphens is an extremely unstable feature of English spelling; both writers and dictionaries vary in their usage.

Attributive and predicative n-forms

Here is a list of noun phrases in which n-forms are acting as modifiers of the head. (For n-forms, see Chapter 3, pp. 39, 44.) As with the ing-forms, they are divided into two groups. Group 1 are gradable, and group 2 are not.

1. a broken man
   a disappointed customer
   a justified aspersion
   an expected message
   a tangled web

2. an accused man
   a written communication
   a deserted village
   a married man
   a forgotten expedition
   a printed pamphlet
   a granted wish

All of these, in both groups 1 and 2, are systematically related to each of two sentences like the following. (The difference between the two sentences is one of **voice**; see Chapter 5, pp. 80–3.)

Something breaks the man –
The man is broken by something
Something disappoints the customer –
The customer is disappointed by something
Something justifies the aspersion –
The aspersion is justified by something

Somebody expects the message –
The message is expected by somebody
Somebody accuses the man –
The man is accused by somebody
Somebody writes the communication –
The communication is written by some-
body
Somebody deserts the village –
The village is deserted by somebody

There are, however, some ungradable n-forms which are of a different character. *A failed priest* is not related to *somebody fails the priest*, but to *the priest fails*. (Exercise 11 is on p. 68.)

Complementation of adjectives

Chapter 3 showed that verbs are often followed by a **complement**, an element that completes the construction of the sentence. In *He mentioned the evidence*, *the evidence* is a complement; in *He seems enthusiastic*, *enthusiastic* is a complement. There are also some adjectives that have to be followed by a complement, for instance:

The members are *fond* of their food
Your statement is *incompatible* with the facts
This arrangement is *subject* to change
The children were *aware* of the danger

If these sentences had the part following the adjective omitted, we would feel that an essential part of the construction had been left out: *the members are fond*, etc. It is true that *The children were aware* makes good sense, but that would be referring to a permanent and general mental alertness, rather than to their consciousness of some temporary situation. There are other adjectives that can either have a complement or not have one, according to more or less subtle differences of sense:

The driver was conscious –
The driver was conscious of his duty
The women will be happy –
The women will be happy to send in their opinions

He was mad –
He was mad on pop music
I was intent –
I was intent on finishing the work
Are you sure? –
Are you sure of the facts?

This also applies to n-forms that are used in the same function: e.g. *The women will be pleased to send in their opinions.*

Very often the element that follows an adjective is quite easily omitted and seems only to add further detail to what is already implied by the adjective itself. *He was angry* tells us about his emotional state, but not what has caused his anger. *He was angry about the delay* adds further detail describing the subject of his anger; *He was angry with his partner* describes the object of his anger; *He was angry with his partner about the delay* describes both. It is therefore not always easy to decide whether we are dealing with complements or **adjuncts** (see p. 37). For example, in *He is severe on truancy*, is *on truancy* a complement or an adjunct? Similarly with *He is glad about his promotion* ('What is he glad about?' or 'Why is he glad?'). The matter is one of rather fine detail and would take us well beyond the scope of this book. For present purposes we will speak of all the elements that either define the scope of the adjective, or make it more precise, as complements.

We have already noted certain kinds of adjective complementation – namely, those that follow comparative and superlative adjectives:

The moonlight was brighter *than the headlamps*
The moonlight was as bright *as the headlamps*
The moonlight was so bright *that we could hardly see the light of the headlamps*
This cheese is the sharpest *that I have had for months*

The italicized parts of these sentences are complements to the comparative and superlative adjectives.

One thing that will be apparent from what has been said about complements to adjectives is that they take very many different forms. The examples cited in the last few paragraphs alone show a wide range of constructions: *... of his duty*; *... to send in their opinions*; *... on pop music*; *... on finishing the work*; *... of the facts*; *... than the headlamps*; *... as the headlamps*; *... that we could hardly see the light of the headlamps*; *... that I have had for months*. This variety of forms is a topic of some complexity which will not be dealt with in this book. (Exercise 12 is on p. 68.)

Complemented adjectives used attributively

So far, all the examples of complemented adjectives have been of the type in which the adjective is predicated. For instance, in *The members are fond of their food*, *fond of their food* is predicated of *the members*. The question that now arises is whether adjectives that have a complement can be used attributively to a noun head. If we have sentences like:

> The statement is compatible with the known facts
> The house is convenient for parties

can we construct corresponding noun phrases in which *compatible with the known facts*, and *convenient for parties* are attributive to *statement* and *house*? The simple answer is 'no'; there are no such noun phrases as: **a compatible with the known facts statement*, or **a convenient for parties house*.

However, this answer does not tell the whole truth since there is sometimes the possibility of placing the attributive adjective in front of the head and the complement to the adjective after the head:

> a convenient house for parties

It is not always possible to resort to this construction. Thus, we cannot say: ** a compatible statement with the known facts*, or ** a conscious driver of his duty*.

We cannot explore all the details of this area of English grammar now. We will content ourselves with two lists of examples (neither of them exhaustive) to show that complementation of attributive adjectives is sometimes, but not always, possible. It also shows, in examples *a, c* and *e* (the asterisked items), that the relation between the attributive and the predicative constructions is not simple, since one cannot always derive one from the other.

1 Predicative adjective with complement:
   a The director is familiar with the figures
   b The house is convenient for parties
   c *The decision was foolish to take
   d The chair is luxurious to sit in
   e The box is heavier than the table
   f This box is heavier than that one
   g This box is the heaviest in the room

2 Attributive adjective with delayed complement:
   a *a familiar director with the figures
   b a convenient house for parties
   c a foolish decision to take
   d a luxurious chair to sit in
   e *a heavier box than the table
   f a heavier box than that one
   g the heaviest box in the room

The sort of structure that is suggested for the attributive examples is shown in Figure 20. The expression *heaviest ... in the room* is a **discontinuous** constituent in the whole.

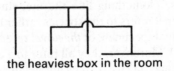

the heaviest box in the room

Figure 20

The comparative and superlative patterns in list 2 are highly productive; that is to say, examples *f* and *g* can be imitated with very great ease. The kind with a to-infinitive (example *d*) is also productive, though there are some restrictions on it which we cannot go into here. (Exercises 13, 14, 15 and 16 are on pp. 68–9.)

Adjective as head of the noun phrase

We have taken the criterial functions of adjectives to be the attributive and the predicative functions. There is, however, another function that adjectives can fulfil, though it is of less importance and subject to very severe limitations. The adjectives in question are printed in italics:

> The *rich* can buy large quantities of freedom; the *poor* must do without it
> The *weak* may not be admired or hero-worshipped; but they are by no means disliked or shunned
> They charge me the same as they charge the *deserving*
> Among the completely *leisured* . . . acute boredom is suffered
> Among the *right-thinking*, the doctrine of the inherent wickedness of concupiscence is still held with an extraordinary intensity

These sentences contain noun phrases as follows: *the rich, the poor, the weak, the deserving, the completely leisured, the right-thinking.* The headword in these noun phrases is not a noun but an adjective, sometimes an ing-form or an n-form. They all have the definite article, which is absolutely necessary, and they all have a generic sense (something like the meaning of *the tiger* when it refers to the species rather than to an individual specimen, or *the novel* referring to the genre). Moreover, they all refer to a class of human beings; *the weak* does not mean weak objects but weak people. This puts a severe restriction on the adjectives that can be used: *the oblique, the hazy* and *the delicious* would be difficult expressions to interpret in this way. Furthermore, they are all plural noun phrases, not singular ones, despite the fact that there is no plural inflection present; we say *the poor are always with us*, not **the poor is always with us*.

Among the adjectives that can be used as heads of noun phrases in this special way are certain nationality adjectives: *the English, the Irish, the Japanese*: e.g. *The English are great travellers*. But not all nationality adjectives can be treated like this; for instance, *American*. This word is, when the need arises, fully converted to the class of noun; it can be pluralized or used with the indefinite article. The following lists show the very different properties of these two kinds of nationality word:

> an American
> two Americans
> *the American are gregarious
> the Americans are gregarious
> *an Irish
> *two Irishes
> the Irish are gregarious
> *the Irishes are gregarious

In fact *American* belongs to a class of words that, although originating from adjectives, have come to be incorporated in the class of noun as well. We can say both *He is eccentric* (treating *eccentric* as an adjective) and *He is an eccentric* (treating *eccentric* as a noun). Other words like *eccentric* and *American* are: *innocent, drunk, itinerant, resident, savage*, etc. Note that they can all have determiners and can all be pluralized. (Exercise 17 is on p. 69.)

Ellipsis of the noun head

The kind of construction that was described in the previous section should not be confused with the kind in which the head noun of a noun phrase is simply omitted through **ellipsis**. Here is an example:

> Such a government combined the aristocratic principle with the democratic

Here *the democratic* is elliptical for *the democratic principle*, as the context makes plain. Reference has to be made to the context in order to interpret the expression. Almost any adjective could be used in this way: *I bought the cheap prints; I couldn't afford the expensive.*

Dynamic and stative adjectives

In Chapter 3, when we studied the meaning of verbs, we found that the great majority are dynamic in meaning; that is, they denote events, happenings and actions which have beginnings and ends and develop through time. But there were a few verbs that denote states of affairs: *He knows the way* describes his state of mind, and we do not find it sensible to say *What he did was know the way*, or *What happened was that he knew the way*.

Adjectives are essentially stative in meaning. They denote static situations, as when one says: *Jack is angry*. Being angry is a state of affairs, even if it only has a brief duration. If we wish to describe a change in the state of affairs, we can say *Jack became angry*. The dynamic part of the meaning is not associated with the adjective, but with the verb *become*. The adjective *angry* still denotes only the state; when the 'becoming' was over, the anger was there.

One thing that is observable about a stative expression is that it does not normally make sense to tell people to 'do it'. Sentences like *Shout to him* (which are said to be in the **imperative mood** – see Chapter 5, pp. 77–8) have the meaning of asking the addressee to take some action. They have to be dynamic to make sense. On the other hand, *Know the way* does not make any ordinary sense, because knowing is not an action. Similarly, with the verb *be* and an adjective we cannot normally use the imperative mood: *Be hungry*.

There is, however, one important respect in which expressions of the form '*be* + adjective' do make sense, and this is if the adjective can be interpreted as referring to somebody's behaviour. *Be hungry* is not sensible, but *Be serious* is. We interpret *Be serious* as an injunction to behave, for the present occasion at least, in a serious manner. Similarly, it is not easy to interpret *He is being hungry*, because *be hungry* is inevitably seen as meaning a state of affairs; but *He is being serious* is sensible provided we interpret *be serious* as dynamic.

Adjectives that have no attributive function

It should now be apparent that classes of words are established in many different ways. Adjectives are not definable by reference to a single characteristic but by reference to a cluster of characteristics. It is because a large number of words have all of the crucial properties that it is useful to recognize the class. (The same goes for nouns and verbs.) It remains true, however, that the characteristics which define the class adjective are not shared by all adjectives. It does not follow that, because a gradable word is used predicatively, people are obliged also to use it attributively. We can say *That man is afraid*, but we do not say *He is an afraid man*. Why not? Well, we just don't. To some extent, words are like people. Each one is unique. It is possible and useful to classify people for certain purposes, but it would not be at all surprising to find that some people are 'marginal' or 'borderline cases'. *Afraid* is a borderline adjective; it has some, but not all, of the features of the typical or central adjective.

Other adjectives that have no attributive function include some that require a complement (see pp. 62–3 above):

> He is loath to put his name to such a document (*. . . a loath man . . .)
> The regulations are subject to alteration (*. . . subject regulations . . .)

Adjectives that have no predicative function

Similarly, there are adjectives that do not occur after the verbs *be*, *seem*, etc. (or, at least, only in a very different sense):

the sole reason . . . (*this reason is sole)
a former filmstar . . . (*the filmstar is former)
a particular book . . . (*the book is particular)
the present king . . . (*the king is present)

It has to be admitted that these adjectives are not gradable; in fact, they have certain features that make them like determiners. They, also, are a marginal type of adjective (though on a different margin!).

Derived adjectives

Here are some common suffixes that occur in the formation of derived adjectives:

-al	conventional, educational, liberal, musical
-ial	menial, official, professorial
-ual	casual, sensual
-able	accountable, desirable, reliable, respectable
-ible	edible, horrible, tangible
-an	republican, Rumanian
-ian	civilian, Canadian
-ant	militant, pleasant, vacant
-ent	abhorrent, decent, diligent, excellent, innocent, succulent
-ate	considerate, delicate, moderate, private, subordinate
-ed	spirited, talented, fair-headed
-ar	circular, popular, vulgar, vehicular
-ic	academic, cubic, domestic, logarithmic
-atic	charismatic, emphatic
-ive	active, co-operative, impulsive, legislative, persuasive, sensitive
-ous	grievous, marvellous, pompous, ponderous, villainous
-eous	courteous, erroneous
-ious	delicious, injurious, odious, religious
-uous	arduous, strenuous
-ese	Chinese, Japanese
-ful	cheerful, dreadful, lawful, wonderful
-less	cheerless, lawless, stainless, spotless
-ish	childish, peevish, Spanish, squeamish
-ly	earthly, friendly, manly, orderly, stately
-some	handsome, fulsome, irksome, loathsome
-y	cloudy, dirty, drizzly, sandy, spicy, tasty

Many of the suffixes listed can be detached from their stems to leave words that exist in their own right. For instance, *-ous* can be detached from *pompous* to leave *pomp*. In other cases, the stem remaining is identifiable with an existing word only after some adjustment of form. Thus, *-ese* can be detached from *Chinese* to leave *Chin-*, which is obviously identifiable with *China*; similarly, the stem of *arduous* is identifiable with the stem of *ardour*. There are some cases, however, where the stem remaining after the suffix is removed is scarcely recognizable as an independent item in the present-day language. *Squeamish* is not related to an item **squeam*, nor is *handsome* related to *hand*, nor *edible* to **ed*.

Some of the patterns of stem + suffix are highly productive. If you take a transitive verb (see Chapter 5, p. 72) like *wash*, or *read*, it is generally possible to add the suffix *-able* to form an adjective: *washable*, *readable*, etc. We would expect there to be a very large number of such words in a comprehensive dictionary. But even if a word such as *pushable* is not in a dictionary, we still know that it is legitimate. We do not need a dictionary to tell us whether it exists. It does not need to 'exist'; we can make it up and nobody will notice anything odd.

This does not mean to say that all words in *-able* are analysable as 'transitive verb + suffix' with the meaning 'able to be x-ed'. Quite a lot of existing words are formed on a different pattern; *amiable* is not formed from an independently existing verb, and *fashionable* is not formed on the verb *to fashion*, but on the noun *fashion*. All that is claimed is that 'transitive verb + able' is a productive pattern.

Other patterns are not fully productive. One can add *-ful* to quite a large number of nouns that denote abstract concepts: *graceful*, *dreadful*, *scornful*, *careful*. But there are limits to what the native speaker of English is prepared to accept. For various reasons, which are not always easy to specify, the following words would not generally be recognized as possible words: **speechful*, **failureful*, **senseful*, **meditationful*, **angerful*, **flairful*, **calmful*. (Exercises 18 and 19 are on pp. 69–70.)

Compound adjectives

We have already noticed the existence of compound adjectives of the pattern *epoch-making* and *man-eating* (see p. 61). There are quite a number of other patterns of compound. Here is a very miscellaneous list of examples: *far-reaching, everlasting, outstanding, low-slung, homemade, highly strung, man-made, even-tempered, even-handed, whole-hearted, hand-written, aboveboard, foolhardy, full-scale, up-market, lightweight, last-minute, second-hand, well-off, roundabout*. It can be seen that many of these adjectives have an ing-form or an n-form as their second element. (Exercise 20 is on p. 70.)

Exercises

Exercise 1

What verbs could you use to fill the space left in these sentences? Suggest several verbs for each sentence.

> The soup —— delicious
> The music —— modern
> Those photographs —— interesting
> The crowd —— hostile

Exercise 2

Take the sentences you have written for Exercise 1 and make a list of at least twelve words that could be used as modifiers in front of the adjectives. For example, the word *very* might be included since we could have *The music was modern* and *The music was very modern*.

Exercise 3

Which of these adjectives have regular comparative and superlative forms; which have irregular ones and which have none at all? Arrange the inflectable ones and the uninflectable ones in two columns.

> confidential, powerful, hard, lively, pure, harmful, clever, small, light, free, dirty,

hollow, active, musical, harsh, expensive, sound, dear, tall, cloudy, rusty, friendly, broken, interesting, close, distant, far, near, regular, stylish, unsound, impure

Exercise 4

If you discovered that the following were genuine English adjectives that you had never met before, which would you expect to be inflectable and which uninflectable? Why?

> pesh, regical, omply, jite, beloyable, osty, amless, horge, baint, sirterous, filibate, unjite, insone

Exercise 5

What antonyms can you find for the following gradable adjectives? Which one in each pair is the 'neutral' one?

> deep, narrow, clean, bad, tight, young, light (*in the optical sense*), heavy, ripe

Exercise 6

Do you think the italicized words in these expressions are being used as qualitative adjectives, or as colour adjectives?

> a shocking *pink* hat, deep *purple* robes, a very *green* valley, her marvellously *blue* eyes, a *black* mood, a light *grey* pullover, a *grey* area, a brick *red* building

Exercise 7

What kinds of adjectives are the italicized words – qualitative, colour or classifying?

> These *costly* groups and committees should be disbanded
> They brought on a *splendid Chinese* dragon
> They showed a *natural bureaucratic* reluctance to engage in *public* debate
> This is an *important* part of the Centre's work

The prodution's *visual* surprises resulted
in a *dreamlike* quality
He has a *matter-of-fact* manner
He is a *young black* boxer

burning toast
breaking windows
infuriating monkeys
examining magistrates

Exercise 8

Divide the listed expressions into three types –
1, 2 and 3 – as described here:

1   noun phrase: attributive gradable ing-form
+ head –

e.g. *a depressing performance* (systematically related to sentences like *the performance depresses one*, with a human
complement);

2   noun phrase: attributive non-gradable ing-
form + head –

e.g. *a sinking ship* (systematically related
to sentences like *the ship sinks*, with subject and verb and no complement);

3   non-finite clause: verb + complement –

e.g. *eating soup* (in which *soup* is the complement of the verb *eating*).

distracting signals, corrupting literature,
existing procedures, flowering bulbs, giving evidence, forging papers, winning side,
tinkling cymbal, awaiting burial, invading
forces, crushing blows, escaping detection, lying stories, rising tide, reclaiming
prisoners, amusing lyrics, taking exercise,
bulging eyes

If you insert the definite article into the listed
examples, this will help to distinguish one of the
types from the other two: e.g. *the distracting
signals* v. *giving the evidence* (not **the giving
evidence*).

Exercise 9

Put each of the following expressions into two
sentences to show that they have two different
structural interpretations:

Exercise 10

The following examples are not ambiguous like
those given in the previous examples. Why not?

burning some toast
an examining magistrate
understanding traffic
laughing children
interesting books

Exercise 11

Which of these noun phrases is relatable to a
subject + verb construction and which to a verb
+ complement construction?

a convicted murderer
some fallen stones
the vanished light
a painted surface

Exercise 12

Write sentences in which there is a predicative
adjective that is complemented by the following
expressions. For instance, if the expression is *of
the lions*, you could write *Daniel was not afraid
of the lions*. (NB   Take care that it really is an
adjective that you use; for instance, *Daniel
complained of the lions* would not do, since
complained is a verb not an adjective.)

at making coffee
with her new job
that it would have merited dismissal
to speak to the people who had been
absent

Exercise 13

Which of the following sentences can be converted into noun phrases like those in list 2
(p. 63)?

The events were easy to photograph

That material is suitable for the purpose

The car is longer than the trailer

Your health is better than mine

These people are glad of your help

That man is unreasonable about getting time off

This type of car is liable to heavy running costs

The river is the longest in this part of the country

This chair is comfortable for sitting at table

The organizer is uncertain of his aims

Exercise 14

1 Write sentences containing the following combinations of adjective and noun, but add a complement after the noun; for instance, for *nice people* one could write *They are nice people to visit*.

2 Convert each sentence into the corresponding pattern where the adjective is predicative: e.g. *The people are nice to visit*. Are there any cases where the second sentence seems, in your judgement, odd or unacceptable (e.g. **the decision was foolish to take*)?

> dangerous roof, alarming scene, important facts, useful people, easy garden, boring programmes, thoughtless words, laborious hill, ineffective measures, harmful leaves, difficult typewriter, big house, permissible door

Exercise 15

Turn to the passage of journalistic text quoted in Exercise 27 on p. 35. List the adjectives and decide whether they are used in a gradable or an ungradable sense. Include any adjectival ing-forms and n-forms.

Exercise 16

This is an exercise in which you can do a little comparative research. Take a passage of arts criticism from a newspaper and another passage of current affairs reporting (about 200 words each). List the adjectives – including any ing-forms or n-forms – that are used in typical adjectival functions. (NB Take care not to include any nouns; e.g. *a delicate Dixieland style* has the adjective *delicate* and the noun *Dixieland* as modifiers of *style*.)

What proportion of the adjectives is gradable in each of the passages?

Exercise 17

Which type of word do the following adjectives belong to – the same type as *Irish*, or the same type as *American*?

> Spanish, Chinese, French, German, Swedish, Norwegian, Russian, Australian, Portuguese, Swiss

Exercise 18

Are there possible adjectives in *-ful* based on the following nouns? After you have reached a decision, look them up in a dictionary to see if they are there. For those that cannot have *-ful* added, are there any other suffixes that could be used to form an adjective?

> ease, mind, cause, fancy, sight, deceit, solace, fault, trash, waste, symbol, insight

Exercise 19

What adjectives can you find that are formally related to the following words? (e.g. *graceful* is related to *grace*, and *hypothetical* is related to *hypothesis*; also, *sharp* is related to *sharpness* by the subtraction of a suffix.) Note what sort of word it is that you start with (e.g. *grace*, *hypothesis* and *sharpness* are all nouns). (NB Do not include ing-forms and n-forms.)

> taste, flavour, thought, reason, logic, concept, theory, imagine, soap, explode, problem, historic, wife, tyrant, statue, accent, satire, govern, fame, sincerity,

saltiness, salt, weep, truth, respect, legalize, widen, shame, virtue, hunger, custody, trouble

Exercise 20

Here is a further exercise rather like that in Chapter 1 (p. 17) on the distributional classification of words. This time some of the words belong to more than one class. Classify the words and name the classes:

answer, dwindle, manage, prolific, secret, arrive, emerge, outstanding, provide, show, cause, pilgrim, recent, song, daily, original, save, take, welcome

Here is the frame in which to test the distribution of the words:

The	A welcome	that	B please-	s	C bring-	s	the	D pious	E answer

5 Sentences

Basic sentence patterns

In Chapter 3 (pp. 36–7) we saw that a sentence consists of a subject and a verb, and perhaps other elements following the verb. If other elements are necessary to complete the structure of the sentence, they are called complements; and if they are 'optional extras', giving circumstantial detail, they are called adjuncts. The following examples illustrate these types of structure. Group 1 has no complement and no adjunct, just subject and verb. Group 2 has subject, verb and complement. Group 3 has subject, verb and adjunct. Group 4 has subject, verb, complement and adjunct. The boundaries between the sentence elements are marked with a vertical stroke.

1   The last train | has arrived
    Bill | drives
    She | was writing
2   Your uncle | left | a message
    They | are demolishing | a building
    The councillors | seem | very determined
    Bill | has been | a postman
3   The last train | has arrived | already
    Bill | drives | quite expertly
    She | was writing | in the library
4   Your uncle | left | a message | yesterday
    They | are demolishing | a building | with some dynamite

The councillors | seem | very determined | this week
Bill | has been | a postman | all his working life

Most of the elements of which these sentences consist belong to the types of phrase we have been looking at in Chapters 2, 3 and 4. Thus, for example, *the last train* is a noun phrase; *are demolishing* and *seem* are verb phrases; *in the library* is a prepositional phrase. In group 4, *very determined* is an adjective phrase, and so on. One or two of the sentence elements are phrases of a type we have not yet studied, e.g. *already*, *yesterday* and *quite expertly*. These are **adverb phrases**. They will be dealt with later in this chapter (p. 74). In the sentences listed above, these adverb phrases are functioning as adjuncts.

For the present we shall not pay any further attention to adjuncts. If they are left out of a sentence, the character of the structure remaining is not affected. Therefore, if we want to study the fundamentals of sentence structure, it is preferable not to include adjuncts. They can always be added on to the basic patterns afterwards.

It would take us beyond the scope of this book to make a close study of all the types of sentence and to compare and contrast them in detail. We must content ourselves with listing the few simplest and most sharply differentiated kinds and pass over the complex, problematic and marginal types. So let us set up six types of sentence pattern, as follows:

1 With no complement (subject + verb):

The car crashed

2 With a **transitive** complement – also known as an **object** (subject + verb + object):

John smashed the windscreen

3 With two transitive complements, known as **indirect object** and **direct object** (subject + verb + indirect object + direct object):

John gave the children some food

4 With an **ascriptive complement**, also known simply, if confusingly, as 'complement' (subject + verb + complement):

John seems happy

5 With a **place complement**, which unfortunately has no traditional name (subject + verb + place complement):

John is at the office

6 With a transitive complement and an ascriptive complement (subject + verb + object + complement):

John made the children happy

These types of sentence, and the terminology used to refer to them, need some explanation. The general idea of a complement has been dealt with in Chapter 3 (see p. 37), but now we need to distinguish between several kinds of complement, the kind called object, the kind called ascriptive complement, and the kind called place complement.

Objects

Objects are elements that refer to participants distinct from the subject of the sentence. The verb *smash* allows for two participants to be referred to (i.e. it is a 'two-place' verb; see p. 46); it refers to somebody that does the smashing and a thing that gets smashed. We can say, therefore, that *smash* (at least as it occurs in the context *John smashed the windscreen*) is a **transitive verb**, and that this sentence is a transitive sentence; i.e. the 'process' of smashing carries across from one participant in the event, the subject *John*, to another, *the windscreen*. The situation referred to is one in which two separate participants are involved. By definition, a transitive sentence contains an object as one of its elements. The following are further examples of transitive sentences, and the objects are in italics:

Somebody has translated *the poem*
Those headlines deceived *the public*
Jack built *a fine house*

Here is a formal test for identifying an object: we can tell that the italicized elements are objects because we can single them out for use as the subject of a passive sentence that has the same meaning. This process is illustrated below (see also p. 44 and p. 81 for the term passive):

Somebody has translated the poem, *so it follows that*: The poem has been translated by somebody.
Those headlines deceived the public, *so it follows that*: The public was deceived by those headlines.
Jack built a fine house, *so it follows that*: A fine house was built by Jack.

If there is a sentence of the type *The poem has been translated by somebody* corresponding to a sentence in which *the poem* is complement to the verb *translate*, then that complement is an object. (Exercises 1 and 2 are on pp. 86–7.) In the sentence *John hates himself* we have the verb *hate*, which is a two-place verb requiring one who hates and something or someone that is hated. It is possible for the hater and the hated to be the same, but in that case the object has to be a **reflexive** form such as *himself*, *herself*, *myself*, etc. Here are some further examples of reflexive objects:

He seated himself by the fire

She has hurt herself
This car seems to drive itself

Indirect objects

Sentence-type 3, p. 72 above, has two objects. If John gave the children some food, it follows that the children were given some food, and (making a small adjustment by the addition of the preposition *to*) it also follows that some food was given to the children. The verb *give* is a three-place verb and it has two complements, both of them objects. However, there is a difference between the two objects; the one that comes first is the indirect object. It usually denotes a person who is the **receiver** or beneficiary in the process. The second one is the direct object and it usually denotes something that 'passes' (if only in a figurative sense) from the subject to the receiver. The order in which the two objects are placed cannot be reversed unless a preposition is supplied for the receiver: *John gave some food to the children*. The preposition is not always *to*; sometimes *for* is required. Thus, *John fetched the children some ice-cream* changes to *John fetched some ice-cream for the children*. Here are further examples of sentences with two objects. The indirect object is in italics.

John told *the children* a story
That woman is buying *Daphne* some clothes
I'm digging *you* a hole
The management won't grant *us* any more holiday
They have sold *their customers* a lot of rubbish
Mary is lending *the neighbours* the car
She is lending *them* it

(Exercise 3 is on p. 87.)

Ascriptive complements

It is unfortunate that grammatical tradition reserves the term **complement** for **ascriptive complements** alone, thus suggesting that objects are not complements at all. Students of language structure have to be on their guard against misunderstandings arising from the fact that in older traditions there is no general term to mean 'any element that complements'. Recently the term *complement* has been used more logically in the broader sense, as it is in this book.

In sentence-type 4, on p. 72 above, the ascriptive complement denotes something that describes or characterizes the subject. In *John seems happy*, *happy* is an ascriptive complement; it characterizes the subject, *John*, by ascribing to him the quality of being happy. (See p. 47 on intensive verbs.) It is very common to find adjective phrases used as ascriptive complements (this is the 'predicative' use of adjectives – see pp. 54–5). However, noun phrases can function as ascriptive complements too. In the following list, the ascriptive complements in italics are noun phrases:

The festival is *an expense*
His colleagues appear rather aloof
The man over there is *the director*
Everybody seems more interested than they expected
Bill is *the one who telephoned this morning*

The quality of being an expense is ascribed to the festival; the quality of appearing rather aloof is ascribed to 'his' colleagues, and so on.

The most commonly occurring verb that is followed by an ascriptive complement is *be*, but other verbs (e.g. *seem*) also have this potentiality. (See pp. 47, 54–5 for more detail on this point.)

Ascriptive complements also occur in sentence-type 6, on p. 72 above. Here the ascriptive complement is not used in relation to the subject but in relation to the object. In *John made the children happy* the ascriptive complement, *happy*, has the ascriptive relation to *the children*, not to *John*. In fact, the relation between *the children* and *happy* is the same whether it occurs in the sentence *The children were happy* or *John made the children happy*. Here are some more sentences containing both an object and an ascriptive complement:

> The jury found the prisoner guilty
> We think the woman intelligent
> They elected the newcomer chairman of the Board
> He likes his tea very sweet

(Exercise 4 is on p. 87.)

Place complements

Sentences of the kind *John is at the office* have the verb *be* followed by an expression referring to a place. Very often the place complement is a prepositional phrase, but there are certain adverbs that also refer to place. In the following examples, those in group 1 have prepositional phrases as complements and those in group 2 have adverb phrases as complements:

1   The desk is *in the study*
    Your daughter may be *in this house*
    The jackdaw was *on the roof*
    My friends have been *in Spain*
2   The desk is *there*
    Your daughter may be *upstairs*
    The jackdaw was *above*
    My friends have been *abroad*

It will be noticed that all the examples in lists 1 and 2 have as their subject noun phrases with identified nouns. If we produce sentences of this pattern with unidentified nouns as subject, we get some rather odd results: e.g. *A desk is in the study*; *Some water is in the glass*; *Several pigeons are there*. The oddness of these sentences can be explained by the fact that an alternative pattern is favoured when the subject is 'indefinite':

> There is *a desk* in the study
> There is *some water* in the glass
> There are *several pigeons* there

We should note that the italicized element is still the one with which the verb is in agreement (. . . *is some water*; . . . *are some pigeons*). The word *there* is merely a kind of dummy subject that anticipates the subject proper.

Also belonging to what is essentially sentence-type 5 (p. 72) is the kind that has as its subject a noun denoting an event. In this case, the complement refers not to a location in space but to a location in time.

> The meeting was *at three o'clock*
> Her birthday is *on Wednesday*
> The election will be *in June*
> The strike is *tomorrow*
> It was *then*

The sentences listed above with spatial and temporal complements are all stative ones. (See pp. 47, 65 for stative and dynamic.) Whether there are dynamic sentences corresponding to these stative ones would be a matter for more detailed discussion. Or rather, the debate would be about whether the element referring to place is to be considered a complement or an adjunct. For instance, are the italicized phrases in the following to be considered complements?

> The father went *into the study*
> Your crumbs are falling *under the table*
> He sank *into a comfortable chair*

A discussion of this matter would require us to define the criteria for distinguishing between complements and adjuncts in far more detail. We may note, however, that the same problem would arise with sentences like *He threw the hat into the cupboard*, *She would put two lumps of sugar into her tea*, etc. These are transitive sentences in that they have objects (*the hat*, *two lumps of sugar*), but the verbs *throw* and *put* seem to require the use of place complements as well. If this is the correct analysis then these sentences have the pattern: subject + verb + object + place complement. (Exercises 5 and 6 are on p. 87.)

Adverbs and adverb phrases

In the preceding section we noted the existence of certain expressions that can function as place complements, but which were not prepositional phrases, e.g. *abroad*, *upstairs*, *there*, *away*, *above*, etc. There were also time-referring expressions like *tomorrow*, *yesterday*, and *then*. Such expressions can also be used as adjuncts, as in the following:

> The car crashed *abroad*
> John smashed the windscreen *outside*
> John gave the children some food *upstairs*
> John seems happy *there*
> John is at the office *tomorrow*
> John made the children happy *then*

Here the sentences that were used to illustrate the basic sentence-types on p. 72 have been expanded by the addition of an adjunct. (Quite often prepositional phrases are also used for this purpose, as in *The car crashed in Spain*, *John is at the office on Wednesdays*.) The traditional term for these words is **adverb**. The words *abroad*, *there*, *upstairs*, *outside* are 'adverbs of place; and *tomorrow*, *yesterday*, *then*, etc. are 'adverbs of time'.

Another kind of adverb concerned with time is the 'adverb of time relationship' (e.g. *still*, *yet*, *already*, and *any longer*, *no longer*, *any more* and *no more*). Some of these adverbs normally occur at an earlier point in the sentence instead of at the end:

> The car has already started
> John is still at the office
> John hasn't given the children any food yet
> She doesn't work for this firm any more

Then there are 'adverbs of characteristic frequency' like *always*, *never*, *usually*, *generally*, *sometimes*, and *often*. These usually come earlier in the sentence too:

> John is never at the office
> He always stays at home

Many types of sentence can also have 'adverbs of manner' attached to them:

> The car crashed violently
> John repaired the windscreen quickly

> He pronounced the words precisely
> She speaks English perfectly
> He looked at her benignly
> They are working hard
> He smoked unceasingly

(Again, the same function could often be performed by prepositional phrases: *The car crashed with a sudden lurch*; *John repaired the windscreen with great care*; *He pronounced the words in a precise manner*; etc.)

The interesting thing about these words is that many of them are derived from adjectives: *violently* is derived from *violent*, *deliberately* from *deliberate*, and so on. On the other hand, the word *hard* is both an adjective and an adverb without change. These words can be modified just like gradable adjectives, which they strongly resemble. The following examples make this clear:

> The car crashed extremely violently
> John smashed the windscreen more quickly than he smashed the window
> He pronounced the words as precisely as she did
> She speaks English less perfectly than French
> He looked at her rather benignly
> They are working harder than we did

The miscellaneous nature of adverbs

From what has been said above, it can be seen that adverbs are of several types. Not only do they cover a wide range of meanings (place, time, manner, and a few others not covered here), but they have very different structural capabilities. Thus the words *tomorrow*, *then*, *abroad*, *away*, *upstairs*, *there*, *already*, *always*, etc. are not gradable like *quickly* (*very quickly*, *more quickly*, *less quickly*, etc.). In fact, some of these words take little or no modification. How could we modify *abroad* in the sentence *I met those people abroad*? Some time expressions can be expanded: *tomorrow*, *tomorrow morning*, *a week tomorrow*, *tomorrow week*, *a week ago*, *last year*, *this morning*. But the grammar of these adverb phrases tends to be rather special and confined to small groups of expressions.

So what unity is there in the class of words traditionally called adverbs? The comprehensive reference grammar of English called *A Grammar of Contemporary English* (Quirk *et al.*, 1972)† says:

> Because of its heterogeneity, the adverb class is the least satisfactory of the traditional parts of speech. Indeed, it is tempting to say simply that the adverb is an item that does not fit the definitions of other parts of speech. As a consequence, some grammarians have removed certain types of items from the class entirely and established several additional classes rather than retain these as subsets within a single adverb class. (p. 267)

Whether the adverb should be regarded as a fourth major class of English words is therefore doubtful. There is, it is true, an indefinitely large number of lexical adverbs, most of them gradable, like *fiercely* and *unflinchingly*. These, however, are largely derivable from adjectives, ing-forms and n-forms in a rather simple and predictable way.

The other adverbs tend, on the other hand, to amount to a number of different minor classes with limited membership. Small classes like *still*, *already*, *yet* and *no longer* are minor classes of structural words not major classes of lexical words.

The traditional class called **adverb** is thus really recognized by the negative criterion of not being the noun, the verb, the adjective, the preposition, the pronoun, etc. In other words it is what is left over when all the comparatively easy classes have been disposed of. Its miscellaneous nature, therefore, makes its claim to be a single class disputable.

Sentence adverbs

The traditional tendency to throw together everything that is not a noun, a verb or an adjec-

† Full references can be found in the Notes and references section at the end of this book.

tive, and call it an 'adverb' is further illustrated by the fact that the italicized items in the following are also called adverbs:

> *Besides*, they are working hard
> *Incidentally*, he looked at her benignly
> *Hence* she speaks English perfectly
> *Nevertheless* the car crashed extremely violently
> John smashed the windscreen, *however*, more quickly than he smashed the window
> *Lastly*, he pronounced the words as precisely as she did
> *Naturally*, he spoke to her

The **sentence adverb** is an element of the sentence that lies outside the subject-matter of the sentence. Sometimes it provides a clue to how this sentence is to be taken in connection with previous sentences. At other times it gives some idea of what attitude the speaker is taking to what he is talking about. The word *however* indicates that this sentence is to be seen as a contrast to some earlier sentence; *lastly* means that this sentence deals with a point that is the last in some previously announced list; *naturally* means that the speaker regards the situation he is talking about as a natural one in the circumstances. Again we find that there are prepositional phrases, and in fact other kinds of construction, that can perform these functions:

> *In fact* he looked at her benignly
> *In the end* she decided not to come
> *To conclude*, I think we should try
> *On the other hand*, they weren't cheap

Words like *however*, *perhaps* and *nevertheless* generally cannot take any modification and they are used quite differently from the time and place adverbs. So they have virtually nothing in common with words like *yesterday*, *always*, *still*, *abroad* or *benignly* which, in turn, have virtually nothing in common with each other. (It is true that there are some words that can be used both as manner adjuncts and as 'sentence adverbs'; e.g. *Naturally, he spoke to her* v. *He spoke to her naturally*. Only the second means that he spoke to her in a natural manner. The other means that his speaking to her was a natural thing to happen. But this is no more remarkable than the fact that there are verbs that convert into nouns, and adjectives that also serve as verbs, and so on (see, for instance, p. 48).)

Adverbs as modifiers

So far our treatment of adverbs has dealt with the adverb, or rather the adverb phrase, as it fulfils some role in the structure of the sentence. In *He walked rapidly*, *rapidly* is an adverb phrase that is acting as an adjunct in the sentence. But the term adverb is also applied to words of the kind that can be used to modify gradable adjectives: e.g. *very*, *rather*, *extremely*, *somewhat*, *astonishingly*, *quite*, etc. The words *more*, *less*, *most*, *least*, *so* and *as* are also included (see pp. 56–8). Furthermore, some modifiers can in their turn be modified, and all the words used for this purpose are 'adverbs'; thus, in the noun phrase *a far more astonishingly difficult problem*, there is a noun head, *problem*, preceded by an adjective phrase as modifier, which has the adjective *difficult* as head. This in its turn is modified by an adverbial phrase: *far more astonishingly*. *Astonishingly* is the head of this phrase and it has a modifier, *far more*, which has *more* as its head and a modifier *far*. Figure 21 suggests this structure.

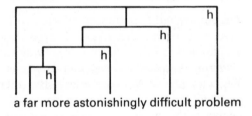

a far more astonishingly difficult problem

Figure 21

Communicative functions

An extremely important aspect of the grammar of sentences is the way in which a sentence can be made to serve the speaker's purposes in interacting with other people. Naturally, a language must provide its speakers not only with ways of referring to aspects of the world about them, but also with ways of letting the addressees know how they are expected to respond to what is said. Thus the difference between *He is finding it enjoyable* and *Is he finding it enjoyable?* is a difference of **communicative function**. The subject-matter is the same, but in one the speaker is saying that it is so, and in the other he is asking whether it is so. That is, the way in which the speaker is involving his addressee in the act of communication is different and, of course, the kind of response that he envisages is different.

Indicative and imperative

Nowadays the term that is used to refer to the various sentence structures that reflect communicative function is **mood**. This is a fairly recent development. Formerly, **mood** was a term that referred only to certain inflectional forms of verbs in particular languages. In what follows, the term will be used in its more modern sense. The main distinction of mood in English is between **indicative** and **imperative** sentences. Furthermore, indicative sentences are divided into **interrogative** and **declarative**. Here are examples of each:

INDICATIVE

Declarative The licence has been renewed.

Interrogative Has the licence been renewed?

IMPERATIVE Renew the licence.

Readers will be able to sense the meaning differences between these sentences, but they might not be able to give an account of the formal differences that produce these differences of meaning. Indeed, the detail that is required for doing this is quite considerable, so here we will introduce only the essential elements of the topic.

In general, the most important aspect of the grammar of mood in English is the way in which the subject is placed in relation to the verb, or whether there is a subject present at all. In the imperative, at least the most ordinary kind of imperative, illustrated above, there is no subject. It is understood that it is the addressee who is envisaged as doing what the speaker has mentioned, but the sentence consists formally only of a verb followed by whatever complements and adjuncts are required:

> Close the door quietly
> Mind your head
> Send me a postcard from Italy
> Give yourself a holiday
> Turn on the television, please

The verb in imperative sentences is always in the base form and there is no possible distinction of tense. Naturally, the speaker is understood to be referring to the present time or to the future, rather than to the past when he says, for instance, *Close the door quietly*. But there is no systematic choice of tense available to him, so there is no point in saying that these sentences are in the present tense, as though they could have been otherwise. Nor is there any possibility of using modal verbs in imperative sentences: **Can close the door*.

Indicative sentences: declarative v. interrogative

In indicative sentences a subject is necessarily present, and the way it is positioned marks the difference between declarative and interrogative. If the subject comes in front of the verb phrase, the sentence is declarative:

> *These papers* are cluttering the table
> *Everybody* has been putting their things here
> *The people in that house* are giving a party
> *He* looks ill

The italicized element in each example is the subject. The reader should try converting the sentences to the equivalent interrogative in

order to see what adjustment has to be made in the positions of the subject and the verb. With the first three examples there is no problem. The first word of the verb phrase is moved in front of the subject. The verb phrases are, respectively: *are cluttering*, *has been putting* and *are giving*. Each of these verb phrases has an auxiliary verb as its first word. The first auxiliary (there is sometimes more than one), is the one whose position relative to the subject gives the clue to the communicative function of the sentence. Thus, the following are all interrogative:

> *Are* these papers *cluttering* the table?
> *Has* everybody *been putting* their things here?
> *Are* the people in that house *giving* a party?

However, the fourth of the declarative sentences above is less straightforwardly converted into the interrogative, for the simple reason that it has no auxiliary verb in its verb phrase. Thus, there is no 'first auxiliary' to move. In such cases as this, English provides a special auxiliary – some form of the verb *do* – merely so that it can be placed before the subject:

> *Does* he *look* ill?

Otherwise, it would have had to be **Looks he ill*? which is not acceptable modern English.

WH-interrogatives

The interrogative sentences referred to in the preceding section are all of the type that are seeking a 'yes or no' answer. *Are these papers cluttering the table?* envisages an answer such as *Yes, they are* or *No, they aren't*. But there is another kind of interrogative sentence that begins with an element such as *who, when, which, which table, what, how, how long, why*. For these interrogatives the answers 'yes' and 'no' would not make sense. They are often called WH-interrogatives, simply because so many of the key expressions listed above have the letters 'wh' in their spelling. This name also distinguishes them from yes–no interrogatives. Here are some examples:

>Where did she put my slippers?
>What was wrong?
>How did you know I was coming?
>Why do you say this to me?
>How much does it cost?
>Which colour do you prefer?

The sort of answer that is required for these interrogatives is quite different from a simple 'yes' or 'no'. *Where did she put my slippers?* assumes that she put 'my' slippers somewhere; it is the specification of the 'somewhere' that is asked for.

Alternative interrogatives

Between the two kinds of interrogative discussed so far, there is a third. The first kind invites the addressee to choose between 'yes' and 'no' – true or false; the second kind asks what information is needed to make the statement true: *She put my slippers —?* The third kind is the alternative question – for instance, *Is he in the house, or the garden?* Here it is assumed that he is in one or other of the named places, so that a 'yes' to the house amounts to a 'no' to the garden. The expected answer is not 'yes' or 'no', but a choice between the limited alternatives offered.

Each of the three kinds of interrogative has its own kind of structure – otherwise, of course, they could not be different kinds.

1   The yes–no type has inversion of the first auxiliary and the subject (*Is he . . . ? Does it . . . ?* etc.):

>Does it rain much in these parts?

2   The WH-type has a 'wh-item' at the beginning, together with the auxiliary–subject inversion (except under a special circumstance not dealt with here):

>Where does it rain the most?
>Who spoke first?

3   The alternative type is like the yes–no type except that the choice of the second alternative is specified by using the word *or*:

>Does it rain, or snow, in the winter?

For the last of these examples it has to be assumed that rain v. snow is being presented as a pair of alternatives. The way the sentence is pronounced makes this clear. If 'rain or snow' is being presented as a single concept, then the interrogative is of the yes–no type:

>Does it rain or snow?
>Yes, it quite often does one or the other.

>Do you want tea or coffee?
>No thank you, I'm not thirsty.

(Exercise 7 is on p. 87.)

Other moods

There are certain other kinds of sentence pattern in the grammar of mood, besides the most important ones dealt with above. These include:

greetings   Good morning, Good night, etc.
exclamations   Isn't it hot!
>What a tall building (it is)!
tagged indicatives   He's clever, isn't he?
>He isn't clever, is he?
echoes   He was at home?
>He was where?
>Was who at home?
>You're worried (are you?)

Moodless sentences

It has been assumed above that the sentences uttered by speakers are all of the kind whose communicative function can be understood, at least in part, by reference to the form of the sentence itself. Unlike these, an utterance such as *That dog*, accompanied by a pointing gesture, has a function interpretable only by reference to the gesture, and probably also the expression on the speaker's face, the behaviour of the dog and all kinds of other non-linguistic factors. The structure of the sentence itself gives not much, if any, hint of the function. Such sentences are **moodless**: neither imperative nor indicative; elements such as verb and subject are not relevant.

Communicative function and discourse

The description of the grammar of communicative functions given above takes account only of the most literal and rudimentary interpretations of the imperative, declarative and interrogative moods. If somebody says *Buy some more petrol*, we know that he envisages the addressee carrying out the action mentioned, but it would be quite impossible to tell whether he means this as a request, a piece of advice, a challenge or an authoritative command unless we take account of factors that are not linguistic – such as whose car it is, and what the social relation is between the speaker and the addressee. Similarly, if somebody says *Your door is open*, we know that he expects the addressee to understand that he is prepared to vouch for the truth of this proposition and, if necessary, act upon it, but whether he is issuing a warning, or a reproach, or some other kind of communication it is impossible to judge without referring to the circumstances in which the communication is taking place. In other words, the interpretation of communicative function cannot be completed by reference only to the structure of the wording that is uttered.

Imperative, declarative and interrogative are grammatical categories, but command, advice, request, reminder, reproach, warning, etc. are categories that belong to a higher plane of inquiry. That higher plane has recently begun to be referred to as **discourse**. Besides taking note of the linguistic structure of the expressions that are uttered (or written), discourse analysis also considers the many factors that make up the **situations** in which people communicate with each other.

Negation

A topic that is rather closely allied to mood is **negation**. It frequently happens that a speaker needs to refer to a situation that is not the case, rather than to one that is. *I am not coming to see you tomorrow* might be uttered as a denial of what somebody has just said, or implied. Moreover, quite often, a negative sentence would be uttered in order to anticipate the addressee's entertaining a false assumption; the speaker has assessed the way the addressee is likely to be thinking and is trying to put him right in advance.

The most usual way in which a negative sentence is constructed is by the use of the negative particle *not* or *n't*. There is an interesting limitation, however, upon the use of this word in that it cannot ordinarily be placed after the main verb; we do not say *He came not, or *He has come not. The second of these cases is easily rectified by moving the particle to where it belongs, after the first auxiliary: *He has not come*, or *He hasn't come*. But the first one does not have an auxiliary. Here, then, as with the interrogative sentences we looked at earlier, we need an auxiliary but haven't got one. English provides the auxiliary *do* to fulfil the need: *He didn't come*.

Using the negative particle *not* is not the only way of constructing a negative sentence. Certain other words have a negative sense inherent in them. These include *never*, *neither*, *no*, *nobody* and *nothing*, as in the following examples:

> I never go on the bus
> Neither room has been vacated
> No apples have been sold
> Nobody turned up
> Nothing will happen

The words that are inherently negative do not always begin with the letter 'n'. The words *seldom* and *hardly* are also negative words. This can be seen by using the following test: A sentence is negative if you can continue it by saying

... *and nor does x*, ... *and nor is x*, ... *and neither has x*, or some such wording using *nor* or *neither*:

> I am not coming tomorrow, and nor is John.
> He never invites his friends, and neither does his wife.
> No apples have been sold, and nor have any pears.
> They gave me nothing, and neither did you.
> The parents seldom realize, and nor do the teachers.
> They hardly ever try, and nor do the children.

If a sentence is positive, the continuation takes the form ... *and so does x*, ... *and so has x*, etc.:

> I am coming tomorrow, and so is John.
> He always invites his friends, and so does his wife.
> Some apples have been sold, and so have some pears.
> The parents often realize, and so do the children.

By this test, it can be seen that sentences containing *seldom* and *hardly* are to be considered negative.

The negative sentences examined above are all finite clauses. It is also possible for a non-finite clause to be negative. In this case the negative particle is normally placed in front of the whole verb phrase, whether there is an auxiliary present or not:

> ... not having been told about the arrangements
> ... with John not arriving until eight
> ... the parents not realizing his difficulty

Voice

A very different aspect of the grammar of the sentence is the contrast between active and pas-

sive voice. This matter has already been referred to (see pp. 44–5 and 61–2). The following sentences are all in the active voice:

> The dustmen will take away the rubbish
> The wind rattled the windows
> The pirates kill their prisoners
> He had acquired his knowledge of horses on the farm

The verb phrases of these sentences do not have the special form that is required for the passive voice: *will take* is active, but *will be taken* is passive; *rattled* is active, *was rattled* is passive; *kill* is active, *are killed* is passive; *had acquired* is active, *had been acquired* is passive. The same main verb is involved in both cases, but in the passive form the auxiliary verb *be* has been introduced and the main verb is in its n-form (or past participle):

				kill
		are	+	killed
will	+			take
will	+	be	+	taken
has	+			acquired
has	+	been	+	acquired

The difference between active and passive voice also affects the way the whole sentence is arranged. When the verb phrase is passive, what was the object of the verb in the active sentence is brought forward into the subject position. Conversely, what was the subject is placed towards the end, after the preposition *by*:

> The rubbish will be taken away by the dustmen
> The windows were rattled by the wind
> The pirates' prisoners are killed by them
> His knowledge of horses was acquired (by him) on the farm

So the effect of the change of voice on the whole sentence is that the order of mention of the two participants is reversed:

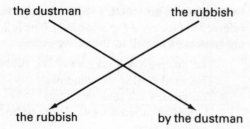

the dustman   the rubbish

the rubbish   by the dustman

The verb that is used to relate the two participants is the same, but the change in sequence correlates with a change in form. Furthermore, the use of the passive form of the sentence enables one to omit any mention of the participant which acts as subject in the active:

> The rubbish will be taken away

What then is the significance of the choice of passive as opposed to active voice? Use of the active voice in English is by far the most common way of organizing the message that one is trying to convey. But sometimes it is felt desirable to mention something early in the sentence. This is often the case when that something is already established as a **topic** in your conversation:

> What a mess we've made. But it doesn't matter; the rubbish will be taken away by the dustman.

In this case the mess is topical in the context, so it is natural to want to mention the rubbish first. On the other hand, *dustman* is a new idea, and it is natural to wish to mention it last. This is the usual way that information is organized in discourse: topical ideas first, new information last. In contrast with the above, let us invent a context for the active version of the same subject-matter:

> We have very good local government services here. Tomorrow the dustmen will take away the rubbish.

Here the dustmen are topical since the local services have already been mentioned, and dustmen are well-known to be local government employees.

The passive voice can also give one a choice of what to mention last. In the above example, the dustmen were mentioned as a new idea. But let us suppose that who takes away the rubbish is a matter of no interest, and that the dustmen are not topical either. So we do not wish to mention the dustmen at all, either early or late in the sentence:

> They're still doing the place up; but it will soon be looking nice; the rubbish will be taken away and there will be fresh paint on the woodwork.

Here the rubbish is topical, and the new idea is that it will be taken away. Who takes it away is neither topical nor new.

Such considerations as these are the chief factors governing the use of the passive voice in English. They are not directly to do with the kind of communicative force of the utterance, nor with the subject-matter, except that sometimes a participant need not be mentioned. It is chiefly a matter of organizing the message in relation to its context.

In conclusion, a word of warning about the passive voice is needed. The voice of the sentence is identified by strictly formal considerations. In order to be a passive sentence the verb phrase must be of the passive form (i.e. containing *be* followed by an n-form). It is not possible to identify passive sentences by means of a purely impressionistic feel for the meaning. For instance, *John received a letter* is not a passive clause. The meaning of passivity associated with the verb *receive* does not make the sentence passive in the technical sense; note that the form of the verb phrase is not passive (*received*, not *was received*). On the contrary, it is an active sentence, and since it has an object (*a letter*) it could be converted into a passive form: *A letter was received by John*. Again, in spite of a certain similarity of meaning, only one of the following sentences is passive:

> The door shook
> The door was shaken

In both sentences, of course, it is true that the subject is affected by the process referred to. But only the second is grammatically passive. The difference of meaning between the two sentences is largely a matter of the difference between active and passive voice; in the second, the action of an agent is hinted at and could have been mentioned (e.g. *by the earthquake*). In the first, no such hint is given and no agent could be mentioned. (Exercise 8 is on p. 88.)

Theme

The choice between active and passive voice is not the only means a speaker has of controlling the way a sentence is organized as a message. In fact there are, in all, three layers of control over the choice of a topic.

First, each verb tends to select one of its participants as the neutral topic. *Jack believed the story* has *Jack* as the subject with the verb *believe*; but *The story convinced Jack* has *the story* as subject with the verb *convince*. Thus, *believe* and *convince* have different requirements about what participant is chosen as subject. Since the subject is what ordinarily comes first, this makes the most normal kind of topic. Similar pairs of sentences can be found:

> We like the house
> The house pleases us

> He owes me an apology
> An apology is due to me from him

> This drawer contains the cutlery
> The cutlery occupies this drawer

> He descried a ship
> A ship came into (his) view

In general it is not easy to construct pairs of sentences like this that have the same, or nearly the same, meaning. This is because there seems to be a kind of ranking order for different kinds of participant. Actors in situations, especially human beings, tend to get prior mention. So *John swallowed the stone* is not likely to be matched by a sentence: *The stone went down John's throat.*

Second, when the verb has been chosen and the rest of the elements in the sentence have been arranged around it, the system of voice (active v. passive) enables the speaker to opt for different arrangements such as we have already seen.

The third device for giving a special perspective to the message is that, within certain limits, the order of elements subject + verb + complement + adjunct can be changed. The following pairs of examples illustrate some of the possibilities.

1 He had used this knowledge to pass himself off as a pharmacist.
2 This knowledge he had used to pass himself off as a pharmacist.

1 The morale of the whole British team could depend on his success.
2 On his success could depend the morale of the whole British team.

1 Some of the pigs, . . . you could sort of just walk through them, but you couldn't go near other pigs.
2 Some of the pigs, . . . you could sort of just walk through them, but other pigs you couldn't go near.†

1 He makes a distinction between linguistic assumptions and language-teaching and -learning assumptions. He divides the latter into priority, procedural and comparison assumptions.
2 He makes a distinction between linguistic assumptions and language-teaching and -learning assumptions. The latter he divides into priority, procedural and comparison assumptions.

The second example in each pair is taken from an authentic English **text**; that is to say, it is attested as having been spoken or written on some particular occasion. It has one of the special rearrangements of the sequence of sentence

† This example is taken from Crystal and Davy 1975, p. 41.

elements referred to above; it can be said to be a special **thematic arrangement** of the sentence. The first version is how the sentence would have been if the special option had not been chosen.

It was necessary to produce attested examples of special thematic arrangements, since the beginning student of language structure tends not to believe in their existence. This is understandable, because very often the motive for using them is that they make a follow-on from the preceding context, and if they are cited as isolated examples they often appear artificially contrived. It should be noticed that in each of the examples cited, the element of the sentence that is chosen for initial position is **anaphoric** (see p. 31). (Exercise 9 is on p. 88.)

Sentences: subordination and co-ordination

Throughout this book the sentences to which particular attention has been given have been simple sentences; i.e. there has been just one configuration of subject, verb, complements and adjuncts. This is the kind of expression to which the term **clause** can usefully be applied. A **simple sentence** consists of just one clause. But clauses can be combined in very many ways to make **complex sentences**. The study of complex sentences would take us beyond the intended scope of this book, but it is desirable that we should conclude with a glance at some of the areas not covered.

In general, there are two ways in which simple sentences (clauses) can be combined; they can be strung out one after the other, each one of them being treated as equal to its partners. This is the **co-ordinate** kind of connection. Opposed to this is the kind where one sentence is involved within the structure of another, so that it becomes **subordinated** to it. The nature of these two kinds of combination can perhaps best be put across by means of illustration. The first example below has clauses of an equal status, and therefore co-ordinated with each other. The second example has a clause which is sub-ordinated to a higher clause, so that in a sense one clause has another clause nested inside it. It is like the difference between a string of beads on a thread and a nest of Russian dolls.

1 Then he touched a spring in the wall and slowly the panelling slid open, and behind it were the steel safes. . . . He twisted a key; unlocked one; then another. Each was lined with a pad of deep crimson velvet; in each lay jewels. . . .

(Virginia Woolf, *The Duchess and the Jeweller*)

2 Personal pride and piety demand that ancestors should not be exposed to public scorn.

In the first example, the connection between the beads on the string is in some cases made explicit by words such as *then*, and *and*. In other cases the connection is made by a mere juxta-position of one clause after another. Since this is a written text, we can tell where the writer intended one sentence to come to an end and the next to begin, because she has used full stops rather than semi-colons for the end of the sentences. If it had been a spoken text, it would not have been possible to place a boundary at the end of a sentence with any confidence. This shows that the grammatical construct called a sentence is indeterminate in its upper limits. There is no saying how many clauses is the maximum number possible nor how inexplicit the connection between one clause and another may be without causing the sentence to come to an end.

A minor word-class that is of some importance in this connection is the **co-ordinating conjunction**. These are, principally, the words *and*, *or*, *but*, *for*, *so*, *yet*. They are words that always come at the beginning of the co-ordinate clause which they introduce. We should notice that the word *then* in the above passage does not count as a conjunction, since it does not have to be initial; we could have had *He then touched*. . . .

A glance at the sentence in the second example reveals that part of it could be extracted and, with only a minor adjustment of form, serve as an independent sentence. The structure is set out in Figure 22. The nested clause is *that ancestors should not be exposed to public scorn*. If we omit the word *that*, this part stands out as a simple subject + verb + complement construction. On the other hand, the

that it is functioning like a subject, a complement, an adjunct or a post-modifier to a head. For example, in *The man who hired a taxi*, *who hired a taxi* has the function of modifying the head *man* (this is an instance of a **relative clause**,

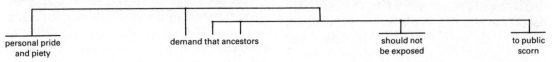

| personal pride and piety | demand that ancestors | should not be exposed | to public scorn |

Figure 22

remainder of the sentence *Personal pride and piety demand* . . . is also a subject + verb construction. The function of the subordinate clause is to act as the necessary complement to the verb.

In order to illustrate further the great range of ways in which a clause may be subordinate, let us take the clause *The man hired a taxi*, which is obviously a legitimate sentence, and see how it can be worked into the fabric of other constructions. In some cases the form of the clause is adjusted to make it fit its new context, but it is still recognizable as being in essence the same clause.

> The man *who hired a taxi* is my brother
> The fact *that the man hired a taxi* astonished us
> *The man having hired a taxi*, he was short of money
> We told you *that the man hired a taxi*
> *If the man hired a taxi*, he must have done the journey quickly
> The journey was short enough *for the man to hire a taxi*
> It is supposed *that the man hired a taxi*
> It was foolish *of the man to hire a taxi*

One thing we may note about these subordinate clauses is that they have no fully specified mood. Anybody who is presented with a subordinate clause can only wait until it gets connected with a clause that is not subordinate before he can assess how the speaker expects him to take it.

Quite often a subordinate clause is integrated into the structure of its context in such a way

see p. 20); it is a post-modifier, rather like *with a beard* in *The man with a beard*. In the sentence *That the man hired a taxi was not very surprising*, the subordinate clause *that the man hired a taxi* is the subject of the whole sentence. Again, *I suppose that the man hired a taxi* has the clause *that the man hired a taxi* as the complement of the verb *suppose*. In *The man having hired a taxi, he was short of money* the subordinate clause functions like an adjunct to *he was short of money*, rather like *for this reason* in *For this reason, he was short of money*.

In the structure of subordinate clauses there is very frequently, though not always, an introductory element which has the function of signalling, 'This clause is subordinate.' There is a minor class of words which fulfils this function, the **subordinating conjunction**. The examples given above include *that*, and *if*; other examples are *when*, *unless*, *since*, and *although*. So we have now noticed two kinds of conjunction. In general conjunctions have the job of signalling a connection between clauses within a sentence. Co-ordinating conjunctions signal a co-ordinate connection and subordinating conjunctions signal that one clause is subordinate to the other.

The details of this area of English grammar are not covered in this book. The purpose of this section is merely to introduce the idea of clauses which are functionally co-ordinated with or subordinated to their context. The reader should turn to more comprehensive and advanced works for a fuller treatment. (Exercise 10 is on p. 88.)

Conclusion: structure and meaning

This book has drawn attention to a wide variety of kinds of meaning, both in the course of this chapter on sentences and in earlier chapters.

1   For one thing, there is the kind of meaning that is describable in terms of the situations that people are referring to when they address each other; i.e. the subject-matter of their discourse. Certain aspects of grammatical structure relate to the situations, participants, attributes and circumstances that one is talking about.

2   Then there are the differences between the kinds of communicative force. The speaker is involving an addressee in one of various ways so that they can interact with each other as verbal communicators giving and receiving messages. There are aspects of grammatical structure that relate to this kind of meaning (e.g. mood, modal verbs and some sentence adverbs – *perhaps*, *obviously*, etc.)

3   Finally, there are differences in the way the speaker's message is being organized as verbal texture. At a given stage in the developing discourse, certain ideas are treated as topical, and other ideas are presented as new information for the addressee. Also, the logical connection between what is being said now and what was said earlier must be made clear enough to the addressee. Moreover, the things that are being talked about must be satisfactorily identified to ensure that the addressee gets the right message. Again, there are structural correlates of this kind of meaning (voice, thematic arrangement, anaphora, connective sentence adverbs).

Roughly we can think of these kinds of meaning as:

1   content, or **referential meaning**
2   **communicative force**
3   **textual organization**

Most sentences are structured in such a way that all these kinds of meaning are signalled simultaneously. A great deal of use is made in language analysis of categories of language **function** such as these, though different analysts come up with different sets of categories. It is obvious that language is socially functional, but it is less obvious how it contrives, in detail, to fulfil its functions, and how meaning gets encoded and decoded in situations of language use.

This book has attempted to introduce the reader to some of the most essential structural categories of English, while not neglecting to point out that structure correlates – directly or indirectly – with meaning, and that the meaningfulness of language is what gives the subject of English grammar its interest. (Exercise 11 is on p. 88.)

Exercises

Exercise 1

Try converting these sentences into the passive form. Be careful to make as small a change as possible. For instance, if the sentence is *The boy kicked the ball*, then the answer is *The ball was kicked by the boy* (not *The ball was being kicked by the boy*, which would be derived from *The boy was kicking the ball*).

It often seems more natural to leave out the last element of the passive sentence, e.g. . . . *by the boy*. So you can put it in or leave it out as you like: *The ball was kicked by the boy* or *The ball was kicked*.

> Somebody writes the notices
> They are expecting some telephone calls
> The public soon forgot the expedition
> His employers dismissed every request
> Terrible dreams tormented her
> My friends have invited me
> Charles had taken the walking stick
> She was trimming the lamp

Exercise 2

Which of the following sentences do not have a passive sentence corresponding to them? For instance, a sentence such as *Jack is a farmer* does not correspond to any sentence **A farmer is been by Jack*. For those sentences that do have a passive equivalent, write it out.

He will keep it
I had better warm the pudding
He got impatient
You must not swear
The trouble is beginning
They took her away
They have brought the luggage to her
The landlord told me
The food is in the kitchen
The floor is yours
I'm going home

Exercise 3

Take the sentences listed on p. 70 (first column) and write them down in three other ways:

1 Change the order of the two objects and supply a preposition (e.g. *John told a story to the children*);
2 Put the receiver into subject position in a passive version of the sentence (e.g. *The children were told a story*);
3 Give another passive version but with the thing transferred (e.g. *a story*) in subject position, and supply a preposition for the receiver (e.g. *A story was told to the children*).

Exercise 4

With which of these verbs could you write a sentence of type 3 (see p. 72) and with which a sentence of type 6? (NB Some verbs can be used in both patterns.)

> tell, throw, leave, owe, consider, make, call, think, find, save, declare

Exercise 5

Sort out the following sentences into the six types listed on p. 72. (Some of them have adjuncts, which should be ignored when classifying the sentences.)

1 His work is professional
2 They can keep the change
3 I consider her perfect
4 The sun is setting
5 The landlord is away
6 I've brought you a cup of tea
7 He failed miserably
8 She is a flower girl at present
9 They might send me an invitation
10 The jury found her innocent after two hours
11 He is behind the curtain
12 She is absolutely perfect

Exercise 6

The sentences in Exercise 5 were extremely short and simple. Most real sentences are more complex because at least one of the items that act as subjects, complements and adjuncts are considerably longer. Here are some more difficult examples. Distinguish the different sentence types.

1 Every movement expresses her furious resolution.
2 She's done it at the first shot.
3 Nearly everybody else in the cast had learnt their lines.
4 The jury's decision was a just solution to the case.
5 The man from the office read us a very short message in a stifled voice.

Exercise 7

What is the mood of these sentences? Say whether they are declarative, yes–no interrogative, WH-interrogative, alternative interrogative, or imperative.

1 That is my chair.
2 Is that my chair?
3 Is that your chair or mine?
4 What is that?
5 You have brought your daughter up too strictly.
6 What do you really think?
7 Sit down, Miss Tudor.
8 When did you finish the work?
9 Did Eliza tell you that?

10 Who did you see at the meeting?
11 Don't forget your coat.
12 Was the language French or German?
13 There were a hundred or so pieces of paper on the floor.
14 Would you like another piece of cake?

Exercise 8

Which of these sentences are passive?

1 The patient underwent an operation.
2 The door slammed in the wind.
3 This paint spreads evenly.
4 Incalculable damage had been done.
5 The stable was damaged by the hurricane.
6 The decorator daubed the wall with paint.
7 The wall was daubed with paint by the decorator.
8 An operation was undergone by the patient.
9 The door was slammed by the wind.

Exercise 9

Decide what the sequence of elements is for each of these sentences:

> This knowledge he had used
> On his success could depend their morale
> Other pigs you couldn't go near
> The latter he divides as follows
> Over there live my parents
> His crimes he kept secret

Exercise 10

In the following sentences the italicized clause is either a subject, a complement, an adjunct or a post-modifier to a head. Decide which it is in each case.

1 *When they wanted to go out*, they had to ask permission.
2 He reported *that the lights were out*.
3 The train *that we wanted to catch* has just left.

4 He is on the train *that we wanted to catch*.
5 *That he was so ill* shocked her terribly.
6 She was unwilling to believe *that he was so ill*.
7 Please ring me up tomorrow, *unless you are still in London*.
8 *That the door was open* convinced me *that the horse had been stolen*.
9 The horse *which had been stolen* turned up later.

Exercise 11

Examine the way the 'speaker' in the following poem is interacting with his addressee. What remarks could you make about the way the language of the poem affects (or effects) this interaction? (Consider the use of mood, of one of the sentence adverbs, and of person reference.)

I'm Through with You for Ever

> The oddest, surely, of odd tales
>   Recorded by the French
> Concerns a sneak thief of Marseilles
>   Tried by a callous Bench.
>
> His youth, his innocency, his tears –
>   No, nothing could abate
> Their sentence of 'One hundred years
>   In galleys of the State.'
>
> Nevertheless, old wives affirm
>   And annalists agree,
> He sweated out the whole damn term,
>   Bowed stiffly, and went free.
>
> Then come, my angry love, review
>   Your sentence of today.
> 'For ever' was unjust to you,
>   The end too far away.
>
> Give me four hundred years, or five –
>   Can rage be so intense? –
> And I will sweat them out alive
>   To prove my impenitence.

(Robert Graves, *Poems 1953*)

Glossary

accent a system of pronunciation associated with a group of speakers from a particular class or region (e.g. an upper-class accent, a West-Country accent).

active see **voice**.

adjective one of the major word classes; adjectives can function as head of a phrase attributive to a noun (e.g. *a small house*) or predicated of a subject (e.g. *the house is small*). Many adjectives are **gradable**.

adjective phrase a class of expressions containing an adjective as head, with or without modifiers; e.g. *very cheap, comfortable, good to the neighbours*.

adjunct an element in the structure of sentences. Adjuncts are appended as extras to the essential elements of the sentence. The term is also used (but not in this book) in a more general sense to mean an appended element in structures other than sentences.

adverb the term traditionally applied to a large number of rather different classes of words, including those derived from adjectives by the suffixation of *-ly* (e.g. *beautifully*). See pp. 74–6 for adverbs of place, time, frequency and manner, and pp. 76–7 for 'sentence adverbs'.

adverbial

1 an element in the structure of sentences roughly equivalent to **adjunct**.

2 a class of expressions, including **adverb phrases** and prepositional phrases, capable of acting as adjuncts and also in other ways. The term (a noun) is sometimes used without it being clear whether it means 1 or 2. It is not used in this book.

adverbial particle

1 an element in the structure of sentences, closely associated with a verb, which it complements without affecting its status as a transitive or intransitive verb: e.g. *send off*; *come back*; *pick out*; *turn round*.

2 the class of words that can function in this way: *off, back, out, round, over, up,* etc. (See also **particle**.)

affix an element in the structure of a word; it is added to the stem for the purpose of inflection or derivation. **Prefixes** come in front of the stem (e.g. *sub-* in *submerge*) and **suffixes** come after the stem (e.g. *-less* in *hopeless*).

agreement the marking of an expression to agree with another expression for the same category: e.g. in *this college* v. *these colleges* the words *this* and *these* agree with the number (singular or plural) of the noun they modify; in *I come* v. *he comes* the form of the verb, *come* or *comes*, agrees with the subject for person and number. (Also called **concord**.)

anaphora the use of an expression to refer to something preceding it in the text, e.g. *she* may refer back to somebody mentioned a moment before, or the expression *a smaller* *house* may imply that some other house has been mentioned already. Such expressions are **anaphoric**. (See also **substitution**.)

antonym   antonyms are words (usually adjectives) of 'opposite' meaning. It would be contradictory to say that something was both *hot* and *cold*. But since there is a middle ground between the extremes, saying that something is not hot does not imply that it is cold (and vice versa). (NB Certain other kinds of oppositeness, like *husband* and *wife*, and *married* and *single*, do not have the same features and are not antonyms.)

appropriateness   the suitability of some expression, long or short, to the purpose the speaker has in using it. Appropriateness is determined by convention and by practicality. As a criterion for describing speakers' success in communicating, appropriateness is superior to the traditional criterion of correctness, which it has superseded.

article   see **indefinite** and **definite**.

ascriptive   an ascriptive complement is an element in the structure of sentences which ascribes an attribute to a subject; e.g. 'The house is *very small*'. (See **complement** and pp. 73–4.)

attributive   one of the principal functions of adjectives, or rather of adjective phrases. An attributive modifier is an element in the structure of a noun phrase: e.g. *a small house*.

auxiliary verb   an element in the structure of a verb phrase which precedes the main verb. The verbs able to function as auxiliaries are *have*, *be*, *do* and the modal verbs.

back reference   same as **anaphora**.

base form   the uninflected form of a word, usually used of verbs.

case   the category for which nouns and pronouns are inflected in order to show their syntactic relation to the rest of the sentence or phrase in which they occur. In English, nouns are inflected for genitive case (e.g. *boy* v. *boy's*), and personal pronouns are inflected for several other cases as well (see Figure 11 on p. 29). See also **common**.

category   any classification of words or other expressions used in the description of the linguistic system of the language. The term is used both for a field of classification (e.g. number, or tense), and for the classes within that field (e.g. singular, and plural number, or past and present tense). See also **term**.

classifier   one of the functions that an adjective may have when it is modifier of a noun head. Classifiers are placed after **qualitative modifiers** (e.g. 'extensive *financial* assistance') and are not gradable.

clause   a structure consisting of the elements subject, verb, complement and adjunct, or a selection of these; a simple sentence contains just one clause and hence the term sentence is often used in the same sense as *clause*. See also **sentence**.

collective   within the category of number, collective number is where the noun is not formally plural, but is treated as plural in subject–verb agreement: e.g. *The team are despondent*.

common

1   common nouns are a class of nouns able to be modified by a wide range of determiners, and having denotational meaning; opposed to **proper** nouns (e.g. *desk*, as opposed to *Henry*).

2   in the category of **case**, applied to nouns, the common case is the uninflected one (e.g. *boy*); it is opposed to the genitive case (e.g. *boy's*).

communicative force   the aspect of meaning connected with the way a speaker is involving himself and his addressee in an act of communication. See also **communicative function**.

communicative function   a classification of utterances according to their communicative force; question, statement, injunction, advice, invitation, warning, etc. are different communicative functions.

comparative

1   a comparative adjective is one that is inflected for the comparative degree, e.g. *taller*.

2 a comparative adjective phrase is one that has a comparative adjective or one of the modifiers *more, less, as,* or *so* (with or without a complement), e.g. *more/less expert (than Jim); as expert (as Jim); so expert (that Jim can't touch him).*

comparison a category applied to gradable adjectives in which the terms are: absolute (not compared), **comparative** and **superlative** e.g. *attractive, more attractive, most attractive.* (*See* **degree**.)

complement

1 one of the types of element within the structure of the clause, or simple sentence; namely, an element additional to the subject and the verb which is essential to the completion of the construction. There are several types of complement including **objects** and **ascriptive complements**. A clause may have more than one complement. (NB There is a tradition which uses the term 'complement' of ascriptive complements only and has no inclusive term for all complementing elements.)

2 an element in post-modifier position necessary for the completion of the structure of an adjective phrase: e.g. *fond of their children; the best in the town.*

complex sentence

1 a sentence containing more than one clause, whether these are **co-ordinate** with each other or one is **subordinate** to another, or both.

2 a sentence containing at least two clauses, one of which is subordinate to the other. (These two definitions may be in conflict with each other but both usages are current, sometimes within the same book. In this book only sense 1 is used.)

composition a process whereby a new word is created by the combining of two stems; e.g. *cross + tree = crosstree.* Words resulting from this process are called compound words.

compound a term to describe the structure of any expression which is made up of parts (usually two) of the same type; especially applied to the structure of words, but also sometimes applied to sentences consisting of co-ordinate clauses (see also **complex sentence**).

concord same as **agreement**.

conjunction

1 the element used to attach one clause to another to form a complex sentence. The conjunction is **co-ordinating** or **subordinating** according to whether the clause is co-ordinated or subordinated.

2 the class of words used for this purpose. Co-ordinating conjunctions include *and, or, but, yet, for* and *so*. Subordinating conjunctions are of various types: *that; if, unless, when, since, although, until . . .* ; and words like *who* and *how* when they are not being used with an interrogative function (e.g. *He told me who would come / how to get there*). The theory of conjunction is barely touched upon in this book.

constituent one of the parts of which an expression is made up. In typical linguistic structures there is a series of layers of constituency; the total expression has 'immediate constituents' and each of these may in its turn have constituents, and so on until the 'ultimate constituents' are reached. See Figures 5 and 19 (pp. 20 and 58).

construction an expression-type, made up of given elements (see, for example, the basic sentence types on p. 72).

context the surroundings or environment in which some expression is used. The context can usually be divided into *a* the 'verbal' context – the remainder of the **text** in which the expression occurs; and *b* the 'situational' context which consists of the people communicating, and the occasion and the medium of communication.

continuous a category of the verb phrase, requiring the use of *be* as an auxiliary and the ing-form of the next word: e.g. *was sitting, has been trying, is being pushed.* Also known as **progressive**.

conversion the use of a word belonging

primarily to a given word-class as a member of a different word-class; e.g. the use of the noun *pen* as a verb in *He penned an answer*.

co-ordinate   two or more constituents are co-ordinate with each other if they are jointly related to their context in the same way. Co-ordination is *a* the process of combining such expressions; and *b* the structural principle of such combination.

correctness   an inflexible principle for judging the quality of a speaker's expressions, depending usually on *a priori* criteria external to the language itself. Now superseded by the principle of **appropriateness**.

countable   a class of common nouns capable of being inflected for number and of taking certain quantifying determiners (e.g. *several, many, a(n)* and the numerals – *one, two, three* etc.) often called **count** nouns.

d-form   one of the inflected forms of the verb, always occurring initially in the **finite** verb phrase and expressing the past tense; e.g. *tried, came, had*. The verb *be* has two d-forms (*was, were*). Some modal verbs have no d-form (e.g. *must*).

declarative   one of the terms in indicative mood: that which correlates most directly with the communicative function of statement; opposed to **interrogative**.

definite article   the word *the*.

degree   the three terms in the category of **comparison** are sometimes called absolute degree, comparative degree and superlative degree.

demonstrative   the words *this, that, these* and *those* are demonstrative determiners; they identify the referent by means of referring to its proximity to, or remoteness from, the speaker.

denotation   a kind of meaning; the property of large numbers of words which enables them to be used for referring to classes of things 'outside language'. 'Things' should be taken to include substances, qualities, relations, events and concepts as well as discrete concrete objects.

dependent   dependency is a property of constituents. If a constituent is present, or is formally modified, because of its relation to some other constituent, then it is dependent on that constituent.

derivation   the creation of a new word by means of modifying (e.g. attaching an affix to) a pre-existing stem; e.g. *kindness* is derived from *kind* by the suffixation of *-ness* to the stem *kind-*.

derivative
1   a word which originated by the process of derivation;
2   a word which originated by the process of derivation, and which is understood to be structurally motivated in this way in the contemporary language. (e.g. The word *kindness* is a derivative according to both definitions, while it is questionable whether *health* would count by definition 2.)

descriptive   the descriptive attitude towards language is that of the scientific researcher who wants to discover the realities of the language system as actually used in all its varieties. The descriptive worker is also concerned with a description of the properties of text; here a description of the communicative efficacy of the speaker's performance is in order. (See also **text**, **system** and **prescriptive**.)

determiner
1   a kind of modifier in a noun phrase with common-noun head; a determiner delimits the reference of the head (e.g. *the* house, *several* houses). (See also **identifier** and **quantifier**.)
2   one of the class of words capable of fulfilling this function.

dialect   a variety of a language which is common to a given group of speakers. The group of speakers may be distinguished by region or by socio-economic class (or both). Dialects differ in pronunciation, in **grammar** (sense 3) and in lexis.

direct object   an element in the structure of the clause (or simple sentence); a kind of **object** distinguished from an **indirect object**.

discontinuous   a constituent of an expression is discontinuous if it is broken off and then resumed after an intervening expression has been inserted. (e.g. *will . . . come* is a discontinuous constituent in the sentence *He will nevertheless come*.)

discourse   a level of linguistic analysis higher than the level of grammar because it takes as its data not only the linguistic structure of what is uttered, but the social structure of the situations in which utterances are made.

distribution   the range of possible combinations of an expression or a form with other expressions or forms.

dynamic   having, or denoting, movement or development; opposed to **stative** (or static). (See p. 47 for **dynamic verbs**.)

echo
1   a functionally important but neglected category in the grammar of mood; literally, enabling the speaker to echo what another has said in order to invoke comment or explanation;
2   a sentence belonging to the echo category.

element   one of the functional parts of which a construction consists – for example, the subject of a sentence or the head of a noun phrase. Elements collaborate with each other to constitute constructions.

ellipsis   the non-inclusion of an element which can be taken as implied and can be 're-covered' from the verbal context. An expression which is incomplete in such a way is said to be **elliptical**.

equal relation   in the grammar of adjective phrases, one of the terms in the category of comparative degree (namely *as . . . as . . .*); opposed to the **superior relation** and the **inferior relation**.

exclamation   a category in the grammar of **mood**, including sentences such as *What a happy find!* and *Aren't you lucky!*

expression   a word, or string of words, having some existence in the language or capable of being formed by the regular processes of the language.

finite
1   when applied to a single verb, having a subject with which the verb is in agreement and belonging to either present or past tense.
2   when applied to a verb phrase, having a finite verb as its initial word.
3   when applied to a clause, or simple sentence, containing a finite verb phrase.

first person   see **person**.

force   see **communicative force**.

form   *give*, *gives*, *giving*, *given* and *gave*, for example, are the forms of the word *give*. A form is any distinct item regardless of its relationship to other forms.

function
1   applied to the 'jobs' that language is called upon to do in the life of societies and individuals; an analysis of the functions of language may result in such functional divisions as reference, communication and text creation;
2   applied to the structure of linguistic constructions: each **element** has a function to perform in the whole **construction**.

genitive   one of the **cases** of English nouns, marked by an inflectional suffix as in *boy's*. In personal pronouns there are two genitive cases, one for the modifier function and one for the head function: e.g. *my* v. *mine*; *your* v. *yours*; *her* v. *hers*; etc. The genitive case is also often called the possessive case.

gradable   able to be modified by intensifiers (e.g. *very*) or by comparison (*more*, *most*, etc.). Gradability is a property of adjectives when these are being used in a qualitative, rather than a colour or a classifying function.

grammar
1   the system of regularities that constitutes a language.
2   the study of the systematic character of particular languages.
3   a written description of a language system, either including all possible levels (pronunciation, syntax and meaning), or just the level of syntax.

greeting   one of the minor moods having its

own rather restricted set of constructions (e.g. *good morning*, *good afternoon*; *hello*).

head the principal element in a noun phrase, an adjective phrase or an adverb phrase; it is an element which must be present (in non-elliptical phrases) and on which any modifiers are dependent (e.g. *large* in *very large*).

identifier an element in the structure of noun phrases with a common-noun head; it is a kind of determiner and has the function of specifying which referent is being referred to, or **identified** (e.g. *my*, *this*, *the*).

identifying determiner see **identifier**.

imperative one of the terms in the category of **mood**; opposed to **indicative** mood. It correlates most directly with communicative functions such as injunction, command, suggestion, etc. which have to do with decision upon action.

indefinite article the word which varies between the two forms *a* and *an*.

indefinite pronoun a class of words of indefinite reference whose functions are like those of the noun phrase: *somebody*, *nobody*, *everybody*, *something*, *nothing*, etc.

indicative one of the terms in the category of **mood**; it correlates with communicative functions that literally have to do with making assertions. See also **declarative** and **interrogative**.

indirect object the kind of **object** which occurs between the verb and the **direct object** when there are two objects present: e.g. He sent *the girls* a message. The indirect object refers to a recipient or beneficiary in the situation.

inferior one of the terms in the category of comparative degree (namely *less . . . than . . .*); opposed to the **equal relation** and the **superior relation**.

infinitive

1 the plain infinitive is a non-finite use of the base form of a verb, e.g. *see*, *take*, in *They will see one*; *You have seen them take it*.

2 the **to-infinitive** consists of the base form preceded by the word *to*, which is called the infinitive **particle**, e.g. *to see*, *to take*.

inflection the process of modifying the form of a word in order to fulfil various grammatical (rather than lexical) purposes. A form like *man* or *table*, which is not reducible to a more basic form, is said to be uninflected; a modified form like *men* or *tables* is inflected.

ing-form one of the inflected forms of the verb, which has the suffix -*ing* added to the stem, e.g. *taking*.

intensifier an element in the structure of the adjective phrase; the kind of modifier of a gradable adjective head which raises or diminishes the intensity of the adjective, e.g. *extremely tall*, *rather tall*, *moderately tall*.

intensive a class of verb able to predicate a link between the subject and an **ascriptive complement**. The most frequently occurring of these verbs is *be*, (e.g. *The music is modern*) but there are others, as in *The music sounds modern*. Most of the other verbs can be used differently, i.e. not as intensive verbs (e.g. *The waiter sounds the gong.*) Intensive verbs are also sometimes called **linking verbs** or **copulas**.

interrogative one of the terms in indicative mood: that which correlates most directly with the asking of questions; opposed to **declarative**. There are three kinds of interrogative: the yes–no type (e.g. *Have you finished?*), the alternative type (e.g. *Do they prefer tea or coffee?*), and the WH-type (e.g. *Where does he live?*).

intransitive

1 a kind of clause, or simple sentence, which contains no complement of the sort called **object** (e.g. *The weather was stormy*; *The children are playing*; *The train is in the siding*).

2 intransitive verbs are a class of verbs capable of being the verb in an intransitive clause. Opposed to **transitive**.

irregular not conforming to the usual rule but to a special one; thus, the plural of *goose* is formed not by the regular means of adding the -*s* suffix, to give **gooses*, but by replacing the vowel to give *geese*.

lexical having to do with the **lexicon** – the stock of ready-made expressions in a language; this includes idioms as well as words. The lexical stock is increased by various means including borrowing (see **loan word**), derivation and composition. Opposed to grammatical, or syntactic (to do with the formation of expressions that are not 'ready-made').

loan word a word borrowed from a foreign language, and integrated fairly thoroughly into the system of the language, e.g. *hashish*, *masseuse*.

main verb an element in the structure of the verb phrase; the final element, usually a lexical verb, which may be preceded by auxiliary verbs.

major classes the classes of words containing very large numbers of lexical items – **noun**, **verb**, **adjective**. (Whether **adverb** should be included is debatable since in part it is an extension of the adjective and in part a collection of separate minor classes.) Major classes are 'open sets' in the sense that the complete inventory of items belonging to such a class at any one time is indeterminate: new words are easily added for special purposes and may gradually be taken into the established lexical stock.

mass an alternative term to **uncountable** applied to a class of nouns; opposed to **countable** (or **count**).

medium of communication the physical means whereby communication is achieved – speech and writing are the most obvious media.

minor classes the large number of small classes of words that have specialized grammatical uses and generally have very little lexical 'content'; including prepositions, determiners, personal pronouns, indefinite pronouns, auxiliary verbs, and conjunctions. Minor classes are 'closed sets' in the sense that a complete list can be given and new items are not easily added.

modal verb a small class of verbs having specialized grammatical functions as finite auxiliaries. They lack s-forms, ing-forms and n-forms, and have no non-finite uses; some of them lack d-forms too. The words are: *will*, *would*, *may*, *might*, *shall*, *should*, *can*, *could*, *must*, *ought(to)*, *need*, *dare* and *used(to)*.

modification
1 the process of changing the form of a word for inflection or any other purpose; e.g. the modification of *book* to *books*, *man* to *men*, *calm* to *calmness* or *grief* to *grieve*.
2 the function of a modifier in relation to a head; e.g. the function of *the* and *large* in *the large house*, or of *very* in *very expensive*.

modifier an element in a construction containing a **head**; the modifier is dependent on the head and, in one of various ways, limits or slightly changes the significance of the head. Modifiers which come after the head, and which are often phrasal in nature, are known as **post-modifiers**. Examples are:
the machine *in the shed*
the machine *which we have just acquired*.

mood a category of the clause, or simple sentence. It has to do with expressing the communicative force of the speaker's utterance. The principal terms in the category are **imperative** and **indicative**; it also includes **echoes**, **greetings** and **exclamations**.

moodless a term sometimes used for rudimentary kinds of clauses in which the communicative force is not explicit; especially those constructions which have no verb, like *Happy birthday* and *Ticket holders this way*.

n-form one of the inflected forms of the verb, particularly used along with the auxiliary **be** to form the passive (e.g. will be *broken*, was *broken*, etc.), with auxiliary **have** to form the perfect (e.g. will have *broken*, has *broken*), and in various other uses. NB Not all n-forms have 'n' in them. (Also known as the **past participle**.)

negation the declaring that something is not the case; reversal of a positive declaration. Negative and positive are the terms in a category often known as **polarity**.

non-finite the opposite of **finite**. Non-finite verbs have neither past nor present tense, and are not bound to a subject by means of agreement. Infinitives are included among non-finite verbs, and so are ing-forms and n-forms.

non-standard　used of dialects which lack the wide currency and the prestige associated with standard dialects.

notional　based upon an impressionistic account of meaning, rather than on an analysis of the formal properties of language.

noun　one of the major word-classes; a noun (e.g. *farm*) can function as head of a phrase (e.g. *the farm*) capable of acting as subject of a clause (e.g. *the farm is ours*), and in other ways. See also **common** and **proper**.

noun phrase　a class of expressions containing a noun (or a pronoun) as head, with or without modifiers coming before or after it; e.g. *these new houses, carelessness, you alone*, etc.

number　an inflectional category of the noun, in which the terms are plural (referring to more than one), singular (either referring to one, or to something not enumerated) and **collective**.

object

1　an element in the structure of the (simple) sentence; a type of **complement** denoting a participant that is distinct from the subject (unless explicitly reflexive), e.g. *The boy kicked the ball*; *The boy kicked himself*. An object can generally be converted into the subject of a systematically related passive sentence (e.g. *The ball was kicked by the boy*).
2　see also **prepositional object**.

one-place verb　a verb which requires no complement, only a subject (e.g. *Bill snores*).

paradigm

1　a set of related forms; an inflectional paradigm is a set of inflected forms of the same word (e.g. *give, gives, gave, given, giving*);
2　such a set of forms to be used as an example for learners of the language.

part of speech　see **word-class**.

participant

1　one of the entities involved in a situation referred to by a sentence; e.g. in a situation of eating, the participants are an eater (an agent) and something eaten (an affected entity). Participants are distinguished from the circumstances of the situation, especially details of time, place, manner, motive, etc.
2　one of the people participating in the act of communication: the speaker and the addressee(s).

participle

1　past participle: the n-form of a verb when it is used as part of a verb phrase, or in an adjectival function.
2　present participle: the ing-form of a verb when it is used as part of a verb phrase or in an adjectival function (but not, for instance, when used in a noun-like function).

particle　any small word of structural significance, especially the infinitive particle (*to* in *to go*), adverbial particles (e.g. *up* and *on* in the phrasal verbs *smash up* and *turn on*), and the negative particle (*not*).

passive　see **voice**.

past participle　see **participle**.

past tense　see **tense**.

perfect　category of the verb phrase; a perfect verb phrase contains the auxiliary verb *have* followed by the n-form of the next word. (e.g. *has taken*; *will have followed*; *to have gone*.)

person　a category of the personal pronoun containing the terms first, second and third. First person refers to the speaker of the utterance; second person refers to the addressee(s) of the utterance, and third person refers to all entities that are not first or second.

personal　used of words that are modified for the category of person; especially personal **pronouns**.

phrasal　consisting of more than one word; used especially of phrasal expressions that have a function more regularly fulfilled by a single word (e.g. phrasal preposition: *in spite of*; **phrasal verb**: *sit up, put by*; phrasal comparative and superlative adjectives: *more artistic, most artistic*).

phrase　an expression consisting of one or more words which is, however, less than a clause (e.g. *butter, some salted butter, a* *screwdriver*). It is necessary to consider an expression consisting of one word as a phrase if it is an element in a construction where other elements could have been present; e.g. *butter* is just a word when considered as a noun, but in *We used butter* it is a noun phrase that happens to have no modifiers (cf. *We used some butter*).

place complement   a complement which refers to a place or direction; e.g. *He is on the roof*, *He went there*.

plain infinitive   see **infinitive**.

plural   see **number**.

polarity   see **negative**.

post-modifier   see **modifier**.

predicate   see **verb**.

predicated   asserted about a subject (e.g. in *The bus is late*, *late* is predicated of *the bus*).

predicative   used of a noun phrase or an adjective phrase that is a complement to an intensive verb (e.g. *long* in *The journey is long*).

predicator   see **verb**.

prefix   see **affix**.

preposition
1   an element placed before a noun phrase in order to relate that noun phrase to its verbal context, e.g. *by* in *He sat by the telephone*.
2   the class of words capable of fulfilling this function. These include: *above, among, at, before, behind, between, by, down, for, from, in, in spite of, into, of, off, on, on to, out of, over, round, since, through, till, to, under, until, up, with, without*. (The list is not complete.)

prepositional object   the element in a prepositional phrase which follows the preposition itself, e.g. *the telephone* in *by the telephone*.

prepositional phrase   a construction consisting of a preposition and an object to the preposition, which is usually a noun phrase; e.g. *by the telephone*. (Some prepositional phrases have subordinate clauses as their object: e.g. *my arriving early* in *He referred to my arriving early*. But this matter is not dealt with in this book.)

prescribe   see **prescriptive**.

prescriptive   the prescriptive attitude towards language is that adopted by those who attempt to influence usage by prescribing how people ought to speak (or write); the standards applied to this purpose are often rigid and unrealistic (see **correctness**), and fail to make the distinction between **text** and **system**. Prescriptivism need not be based upon unsound notions of the realities of the language system, but it often is.

present participle   see **participle**.

present tense   see **tense**.

productive   a construction is productive if an indefinitely large number of expressions can be produced by conforming to its pattern; e.g. the construction transitive verb + *-able* is productive since adjectives of the type *fingerable* are freely produced.

progressive   see **continuous**.

pronoun   a class of words without denotation which are able to function like noun phrases, i.e. as subjects, objects, prepositional objects, etc. including 1 personal pronouns which are meaningful by reference to participants in the utterance (see Figure 11 for a complete list), and 2 indefinite pronouns which have no definite reference. These are: *anybody, anyone, anything, everybody, everyone, everything, nobody, no-one, nothing, somebody, someone, something*. Also included are relative pronouns, which are not explicitly treated in this book; they are the words, usually beginning in *wh*, which come at the beginning of relative clauses, e.g. *who* in the *officer who fetched the papers*, and *which* in *words which come at the beginning*.

proper noun   a class of words used as names (i.e. 'labels') for unique individuals (not only people but towns, rivers, etc.); syntactically, these function in the same way as noun phrases with common noun heads, but they have very few possibilities of being modified.

qualitative   a qualitative modifier is an element in the structure of a noun phrase; the function is fulfilled by a gradable adjective, with or without modifiers of its own: e.g. *eloquent* and *rather brief* in *his eloquent speech* and *a rather brief telephone call*. (See also **classifier**.)

quantified   the head of a noun phrase is quantified if it has a quantifying determiner to modify it.

quantifier   an element in the structure of a noun phrase with a common-noun head; it is a kind of determiner and has the function of specifying how much/many is/are being referred to: e.g. *a*, *some*, *several*, *much*, *a lot of*, *all*.

receiver   same as recipient (see **indirect object**).

reference   the act of mentioning or speaking about something. A speaker refers to what he is talking about; by an extension of this meaning, the expressions he uses refer to what he is talking about.

referent   an entity referred to by a speaker.

referential meaning   the aspect of meaning which has to do with **reference** to subject-matter; distinguished from communicative force and textual organization.

reflexive   personal pronouns have a reflexive form (*myself*, *himself*, etc.) which is used when repeated reference is made to an entity within a single clause (e.g. *Bill hurt himself*, as opposed to *Bill hurt him*).

register   a variety of a language which is peculiar to certain situations of language use; the dimensions of situational constraint recognized have to do with the role relationships between the communicators, the kind of social action that the communication is contributing to and the **medium of communication** (speech, writing, etc.). It goes without saying that registers merge with each other in so far as the situational constraints are independently variable. NB   The term **register** is also sometimes used in related but narrower senses, to refer first, to varieties of a language distinguished according to the subject-matter which is being treated (see e.g. Quirk and Greenbaum, 1973, p. 10), and second, varieties distinguished according to the occupa-

tion of the speaker (see e.g. Wilkins, 1972, p. 137, '. . . not a matter of subject-matter but of the language used in pursuance of one's job.'). In both these cases register is just one among several dimensions of situational constraint upon language variation. (See also p. 102.)

regular   conforming to a productive rule; especially used of inflectional forms which conform to the numerically preponderant pattern and which are the model for new coinages; e.g. the '-s' suffix for nouns, which would be used if we coined a new noun (say, *brem*: *How many __ have you seen today?*)

reification   the treatment of an abstraction as though it was a real or concrete entity.

relative clause   one of the types of subordinate clause; a relative clause is a post-modifier within the structure of a noun phrase: e.g. the king *who burnt some cakes*.

relative pronoun   see **pronoun**.

s-form   one of the inflected forms of the verb, always occurring initially in the finite verb phrase and expressing the present tense when the subject is third person singular: e.g. *comes*, *tries*, *is*, *has*.

second person   see **person**.

sentence   a construction consisting of one or more **clauses**; in the literature on grammar, there is much variability of usage in the way the terms sentence and clause are related to each other. The tendency is to use the term sentence both for the kind of construction that has subjects, verbs, complements and adjuncts as its elements (let us call it a clause), and for the kind of structure that contains one or more clauses, and which has some overall **communicative force**. It is a **simple sentence** if it contains one clause, and a **complex sentence** if it contains more than one. Thus *We were out when he arrived* is one sentence which consists of two clauses, but if the first clause (*We were out*) had occurred by itself, it might not be called a clause but a sentence (i.e. a simple sentence). Hence the terms *simple sentence* and *clause* are for many purposes treated as interchangeable.

singular   see **number**.

situation   a relation between participants in a combination of circumstances.

1   situation of thesis: the situation referred to as the subject-matter of a sentence.

2   the situation of utterance: the situation in which the participants are the speaker and addressee(s) and the circumstances are the **context**.

split infinitive   a **to-infinitive** expression with some other expression separating the particle *to* from the verb; e.g. *to always go*, *to simply despair*.

spoonerism   the transposition of initial consonants such as *lend a setter*, for *send a letter*, resulting from a 'slip of the tongue'.

standard   a dialect which has wide currency and prestige.

stative   denoting a state of affairs; lacking movement or change; opposed to **dynamic**. (See p. 47 for stative verbs.)

stem   the part of a word to which an affix is attached (e.g. *thought-* in the word *thoughtless*, or *thoughtless-* in *thoughtlessness*), or to which another stem may be attached to form a compound (e.g. *type-* and *-writer* in *typewriter*).

stress   a syllable made prominent by means of loudness, pitch variation, and/or length; we can say that in the word *speaker*, 'the stress falls on the first syllable'.

structure   the pattern of elements that make up a **construction**.

subject   the element in a clause, or simple sentence, whose position in relation to the verb signals the mood of the sentence: e.g. *the book on the table* in the sentences: *The book on the table is mine*, and *Is the book on the table mine?* The subject also requires agreement of the verb in many circumstances (e.g. *the book on the table is* . . . v. *the books on the table are* . . .). The subject has a thematic value, since it refers to the participant that precedes the verb when the sequence of elements is unremarkable (e.g. the verb *please* has a 'phenomenon' as subject – *The book pleased me* – while *like* has a 'reactor' as subject – *I liked the book*). **Dummy subjects** are subjects like *it* and *there* when these words are used to anticipate a more explicit expression to follow. For instance in *It is true that he is here*, *it* is a dummy subject anticipating *that he is here*. In a different construction, *There is a letter for you*, *there* is a dummy subject anticipating *a letter*.

subordinate   usually used of clauses; a clause is subordinate to another clause if it is dependent on that clause, e.g. if it is embedded, or nested, as part of the structure of that clause. The clause in which it is embedded is superordinate, or dominant, to it. There are very many ways in which a clause can be subordinated. (See also **relative clause**.)

substitution   the replacement of an expression by a token expression which 'stands for' what it replaces, with the effect of avoiding repetition; substitutes are most frequently (but not necessarily) **anaphoric**; e.g. the word *one* in the sentence *I have a new one*; meaning, perhaps, *a new car*. Pronouns are also often regarded as substitutes.

suffix   see **affix**.

superior   one of the terms in the category of comparative degree (namely *more* . . . *than* . . .); opposed to the **equal relation** and the **inferior relation**.

superlative

1   a superlative adjective is one that is inflected for the superlative degree, e.g. *tallest*.

2   a superlative adjective phrase has a superlative adjective or one of the modifiers *most* or *least* (with or without a complement), e.g. *the tallest/most expert (of them all)*; *the least expert (to have attempted the task)*.

syntax

1   the arrangement of words and other expressions in conventionally well-formed constructions, (excluding the lexical aspects of sentences);

2 the branch of language study that deals with this.

system   a language system is a set of linguistic elements related by rules of combination and selection, the whole being consistently used for communication.

systematic   belonging to a **system**; hence established, consistent, intentional, meaningful and interpretable by those who are familiar with the system.

systematically related   two expressions are systematically related if it is possible to derive one from the other by a fixed and formal procedure; for instance, *The office is closed* is systematically related to *Is the office closed?* and *The Council finished the work* is systematically related to *The work was finished by the Council*; *boots for climbing* is also systematically related to *climbing boots*.

tense

1 a category of the verb in which the terms are past and present; past tense is realized by the d-form of the first verb in the verb phrase, and present tense by the base form or the s-form (or, with the verb *be*, by *am* or *are*).

2 the term also has a secondary sense referring to other categories that are used in addition to past or present, e.g. the present perfect tense, the past continuous tense.

term

1 one of the exclusive choices within a category (sense 1); equivalent to sense 2 of category; e.g. the category of number in the noun has two terms, singular and plural.

2 in a non-specialist sense, a term is any item of technical vocabulary.

text   language produced in spoken or written (or any other) medium on particular occasions; text is what is actually observable; it contrasts with the **system**, which is the potentiality. NB In general usage, text is a countable noun denoting any body of printed language. There is no term in general use denoting what is here called **text** (except 'language', which is ambiguous since it also denotes the system).

textual organization   the organizing of an utterance or discourse as a verbal message, with *a* various kinds of highlighting of some parts over others, *b* explicit or implicit connections between the successive parts, *c* reference to various features of the context, both verbal and situational, and *d* stylistic consistency.

thematic arrangement   the selection of what to place first in a clause.

theme   the part of a clause which, at the outset, announces the speaker's topic for that clause.

third person   see **person**.

three-place verb   a verb which requires a subject and two complements referring to the participants in the situation being talked about (e.g. *Bill told his wife a lie*).

to-infinitive   see **infinitive**.

topic   that about which something is said; there are *a* 'global' topics which remain topical through paragraphs or longer stretches of text, and *b* 'local' topics which come and go over shorter stretches. The **theme** of a clause is the topic for that clause in particular.

transitive

1 a transitive clause is one that has at least one object.

2 a transitive verb is a verb that can be the verb in a transitive clause. (Opposed to **intransitive**.)

truth value   the truth or falsity of an utterance. If it is raining, the truth value of the utterance 'it is raining' is 'true'; if it is not raining the truth value of the utterance is 'false'. The term is usually used of statements, but it is relevant to questions, since these inquire into truth value.

two-place verb   a verb requiring a subject and a complement referring to the participants in the situation being talked about (e.g. Bill *knows* French).

uncountable   a class of common nouns which cannot be inflected for number and which can be modified by the determiner *much* (including *how much*), but not *a(n)*; (e.g. *butter, water*).

variable word a word which has not only a base form but one or more inflected forms.

variety a language system special to some group of speakers, or period in time, or social purpose; a language usually comprehends many varieties.

verb

1 an element in a clause, or simple sentence, whose function is fulfilled by a verb phrase and whose relation to the **subject** reflects the mood of the clause; a verb may have complements.

2 a class of words whose members act as the elements in a **verb phrase**, inflectable for tense and subject agreement.

NB Because of the important difference between these two senses of *verb*, some scholars prefer the term *predicate* or *predicator* for sense 1.

verb phrase a class of expressions containing a main verb in final position and possibly preceded by one or more auxiliary verbs; e.g. *runs, has run, is running, has been running, having been running.*

vocative in Latin, a term in the inflectional category of case; a noun in the vocative case can be used to address the person it refers to. English does not have a special form of the noun for carrying out the vocative function.

voice

1 a category in the verb phrase in which the terms are active and passive. In a passive verb phrase, *be* is used as an auxiliary and is followed by the n-form of the next word, e.g. *was broken, has been counted, must have been excluded, to be found.* In an active verb phrase this auxiliary, if present at all, is not followed by the n-form of the next word, e.g. *broke, has counted, must have excluded, to find.*

2 a passive clause is one in which the verb phrase is passive: e.g. *the glass was broken by the boys.* An active clause is one in which the verb phrase is not passive: e.g. *the boys broke the glass; the glass broke.*

WH-interrogative see **interrogative**.

word-class a class of words such as noun, verb, preposition, determiner, etc. Traditionally called 'parts of speech'.

yes–no interrogative see **interrogative**.

Notes on further reading

For discussions of the notion of 'correctness' and the status of usage, see Quirk (1968), especially chapters 5, 7 and 8 and Appendix II which is by J. Warburg.

The inevitability of linguistic change, and the social and psychological pressures which bring it about, are the subject of Aitchison (1981).

Most introductions to linguistics contain a discussion and a rejection of 'prescriptivism' in an early chapter. Lyons (1981) is a good example. A book which attempts to bridge the gap between popular and academic conceptions of language study is Bolinger (1980).

Introductions to linguistics usually also contain discussions of dialect and register; for instance, Halliday, McIntosh and Strevens (1964), chapter 4. A small book devoted to the concept of register is Gregory and Carroll (1978). On dialects, see Hughes and Trudgill (1979).

For further reading on the analysis of English grammar, the most useful compendious treatment is Quirk *et al.* (1972), and its abridgement, Quirk and Greenbaum (1973). These contain a large number of references to works on particular grammatical topics. My own book, Young (1980), has a fairly detailed study of a relatively limited area. The amount of overlap with the coverage of the present work has been kept to a minimum.

Crystal (1980) is a useful source of explanations for linguistic terminology and is obviously much more comprehensive than the glossary of this book.

References

Aitchison, J. (1981), *Language Change: progress or decay?*, London: Fontana

Bolinger, D. (1980), *Language: The Loaded Weapon*, London: Longman

Crystal, D. (1980), A *first dictionary of linguistics and phonetics*, London: André Deutsch

Crystal, D. and Davy, D. (1975), *Advanced English Conversation*, London: Longman

Gregory, M. and Carroll, S. (1978), *Language and Situation*, London: Routledge and Kegan Paul

Halliday, M. A. K., McIntosh, A. and Strevens, P. (1964), *The Linguistic Sciences and Language Teaching*, London: Longman

Hughes, A. and Trudgill, P. (1979), *English Accents and Dialects*, London: Arnold

Lyons, J. (1981), *Language and Linguistics*, Cambridge: Cambridge University Press

Quirk, R. (1968), *The Use of English*, 2nd edn, London: Longman

Quirk, R., Greenbaum, S., Leech, G. N., and Svartvik, J. (1972), *A Grammar of Contemporary English*, London: Longman

Quirk, R. and Greenbaum, S. (1973), *A University Grammar of English*, London: Longman

Wilkins, D. A. (1972), *Linguistics in Language Teaching*, London: Arnold

Young, D. J. (1980), *The Structure of English Clauses*, London: Hutchinson

Key to exercises

Chapter 1   Introduction

1   (p. 17)

A	B	C	D	E	F
the	new	cottage	seems	extraordinarily	bleak
a(n)	dark	building	appears	immensely	new
this	dignified	counter	becomes	moderately	dark
every	immense	desk	is	outstandingly	dignified
	large	door		quite	immense
	old	harbour		rather	large
	short	ship		very	old
	untidy	cup			short
	bleak				untidy
1	2	3	4	5	2

Chapter 2   Nouns and noun phrases

1   (p. 31)

	several	those	a	much	most	all	this	the	your
houses	✓	✓			✓	✓		✓	✓
story			✓				✓	✓	✓
anger				✓	✓	✓	✓	✓	✓

2   (p. 32)

	a few many several these those	a	a little much	all a lot of enough most plenty of sŏme	that this	any no sóme her his my our the their your
houses	✓			✓		✓
story		✓			✓	✓
anger			✓	✓	✓	✓

3   (p. 32)

three informations: *information* is uncountable, so it cannot have the plural suffix or a numeral;

much library: *library* is countable, so it cannot have the determiner *much*;

several apple: *several* requires a countable plural, but *apple* is countable singular;

many carpentry: *carpentry* is uncountable, but *many* implies a countable;

enough letter: *letter* is a countable singular, but *enough* requires a countable plural or an uncountable.

4   (p. 32)

Obviously there is no key to this exercise, but the following are examples of sentences that would do:

> *These windows* are difficult to open.
> Have we got *enough tea*?
> Can I have *two teas* please?

5   (p. 32)

my car, *his blodge*, *this reason*, *no triss*, *the information*, *this herp*, *their food*: could be countable (singular) or uncountable;

all carpaw, *a lot of trouble*, *much prose*: must be uncountable, unless *carpaw* is an irregular plural;

a deed: must be countable singular;

few sheep, *these honkeri*, *enough hawds*: must be countable plural, assuming that *hawds* is a regular plural; *honkeri* has to be an irregular plural.

6   (p. 32)

his house (c.), *a story* (c.), *visitors* (c.), *his parents* (c.), *much education* (unc.), *knowledge* (unc.), *skills* (c.), *a monastery* (c.), *the monks* (c.), *arithmetic* (unc.), *farming* (unc.), *fiction* (unc.), *his motive* (c.), *this deception* (c. or unc. according to whether we take *deception* to mean 'deceitfulness' or 'an act of deceit').

7   (p. 32)

a *wise* education policy; the *untidy* house plans; *thick* furniture catalogues; a *heavy* balance beam; those *unprofitable* oil wells. *The adjectives are placed after a determiner, if there is one, and before a noun modifier, if there is one.*

8   (p. 32)

   d   h   d   h
your handbag;   enough leather;

   d   n   h   d   h
this leather handbag;   a lot of notes;

   d   a   h
some large handbags;

    d   a   h
several attractive concerts;

   a   h   d   n   h
stodgy pudding;   a mystery tour;

   d   a   n   h   d   h
a sunny pleasure dome;   much pleasure;

   a   n   h   a   a   h
bright street lights;   happy little children.

9   (p. 33)

to visitors; *for* him; *for* knowledge; *for* want (of skills): *of* skills; *to* a monastery; *for* this deception.

10   (p. 33)

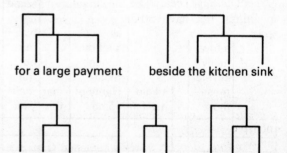

for a large payment   beside the kitchen sink

on your coat   from the tray   into the basin

11 *(p. 33)*

	/s/	/z/	/ɪz/
's'	bits racks cliffs	tabs ways toes	roses ledges
'es'		tomatoes	wishes latches

12 *(p. 33)*

The following are irregular:

cacti (replace -*us* with *i*);

crises (replace -*is* with -*es*, pronounced like *ease*);

salmon (no change);

mouths (change the final consonant of the stem, though not in the spelling);

syllabi (change -*us* to -*i*; but most speakers seem now to treat this noun as regular: *syllabuses*);

phenomena (change -*on* to -*a*; but many speakers now treat *phenomena* as a singular and plural with no change);

mice (change vowel of stem).

13 *(p. 33)*

They get narrowed down in their possible range of meaning: *tins* = tin cans; *colds* = colds in the head; *damages* = specialized legal sense; *youths* = young male persons. The uninflected forms (except *damage*) can all be the singular of these meanings, but have other possible senses as well.

14 *(p. 33)*

1 *the crowd* . . . (*were*: plural) (cf. *was*);
a group . . . (*who*: human individuals; *play*: plural) (cf. *which plays*).
2 *a callous Bench* . . . *their sentence* (not *its sentence*).

15 *(p. 33)*

No key.

16 *(p. 33)*

shoes	common, plural
authors'	genitive, plural
lady's	genitive, singular
ladies	common, plural
teachers'	genitive, plural
Companies'	genitive, plural
Company's	genitive, singular
firms'	genitive, plural
girls	common, plural

17 *(p. 33)*

girl	that girl
girl's	that girl's hat
girls	those girls
girls'	those girls' hats
woman	a woman
woman's	a woman's place
women	some women
women's	some women's jobs
child	this child
child's	this child's head
children	these children
children's	these children's heads
baby	this baby
baby's	this baby's bottle
babies	these babies
babies'	these babies' bottles
wife	his wife
wife's	his wife's head
wives	his wives
wives'	his wives' heads
mother	our mother
mother's	our mother's nose
mothers	our mothers
mothers'	our mothers' noses

18   (p. 34)

The dog's owner has gone away: the owner of
the dog;
The dogs' owner has gone away: the owner of
the dogs;
I found the boy's books: the books belonging to
the boy;
I found the boys' books: the books belonging to
the boys;
I found the boys books: I found books for the
boys;
She is going to wash the baby's nappies . . . : the
nappies belonging to the baby;
She is going to wash the babies' nappies . . . : the
nappies belonging to the babies;
She is going to wash the babies nappies . . . : she
is going to wash nappies for the babies.
(This interpretation may seem somewhat
strained, though in an appropriate context it
would probably not strike anybody as odd; e.g.
*She is going to wash some shirts for her husband,
but she is going to wash the babies nappies*.)

19   (p. 34)

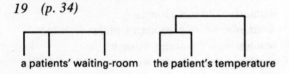

a patients' waiting-room   the patient's temperature

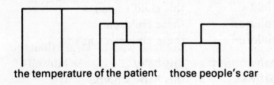

the temperature of the patient   those people's car

20   (p. 34)

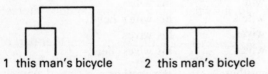

1 this man's bicycle   2 this man's bicycle

1   the bicycle belonging to this man.
2   this bicycle of the sort made for men to ride.

21   (p. 34)

product-ion (n): cf. elect-ion, construct-ion, etc.
(NB   Product *has the structure* pro-duct, *cf*
pro-gress, con-duct, con-gress.)
autocrat-ic: cf. philosoph-ic, graph-ic;
exist-ence (n.): cf. refer-ence, independ-ence;
un-predictable: cf. un-sure, un-safe;
(NB   Predictable *is itself made up of* predictable, cf. controll-able.)
capital-ism (n.): cf. conservat-ism, structural-ism;
develop-ment(n.): cf. govern-ment, depart-ment;
re-write: cf. re-open, re-group;
friendli-ness (n.): cf. sharp-ness, strange-ness;
(NB   Friendly *is itself derived* friend-ly, cf.
home-ly, man-ly, brother-ly.)
impossibil-ity (n.): cf. activ-ity, circular-ity,
advers-ity.
(NB   Im-possible *is itself derived*, cf. im-
mobile; *and* poss-ible *can be compared with*
ed-ible.)

22   (p. 34)

type-writer (n.): type (n.) *and* writer (n.) writer
   is derived from write + er;
snow-plough (n.): snow (n.) *and* plough (n.);
over-burden: over *and* burden; *the latter is
   probably a verb rather than a noun*, cf. over-
   emphasize;
mouse-trap (n.): mouse (n.) *and* trap (n.);
get-away (n.): get *and* away;
baby-sit: baby (n.) *and* sit;
black-board (n.): black *and* board (n.);
wood-cut (n.): wood (n.) *and* cut (?n.);
screen-print (n.): screen (n.) *and* print (n.).

23   (p. 34)

pro-duct   pro-gress   de-script-ion   de-scribe
in-duct   in-gress   in-script-ion   in-scribe
con-duct   con-gress   con-script-ion
               con-script

attent-ion   descript-ion
attent-ive   descript-ive
attentive-ness   descriptive-ness

de-fend de-fence defens-ive defens-ible
of-fend of-fence offens-ive

im-possible	poss-ible	possibil-ity
in-credible	cred-ible	credibil-ity
in-sensible	sens-ible	sensibil-ity
in-describable	describ-able	

auto-crat	demo-crat	bureau-crat
auto-cracy	demo-cracy	bureau-cracy

24 (p. 34)

I; they (people); it (music); they (people); they (young people); I; they (a youth orchestra, *collective number – not singular* 'it'); I; they (the youth orchestra); it (the Beethoven symphony).

25 (pp. 34–5)

The original version was as follows. Other versions might be equally good. (It was a spoken text recorded from the radio, so the punctuation is editorial.)

. . . I've already been told by a colleague at *The Times* that he has already been warned by a source that, if Granada journalists disclose the source – the name of their informant – then he will never get confidential information again from that source, and I'm sure that would happen to thousands of journalists up and down the country.

26 (p. 35)

1 one chair (*numeral*);
2 one has to be . . . doesn't one? (*indefinite pronoun*);
3 one biscuit (*numeral*);
4 a better one (= a better pen; *countable noun substitute*);
5 some fresh ones (*c.n. subst.*);
6 one eye . . . the other (*numeral*);
7 one can't . . . (*indefinite pronoun*); a big one (*c.n. subst.*);
8 one speaker . . . (*numeral*); the other one (*c.n. subst.*).

27 (p. 35)

1.3 *that of the occupant* – what of the occupant? – his interest

1.5 *him* – who? – the farmer
1.7 *the Ministry* – what Ministry? – the Ministry just mentioned
1.7 *then* – when? – after he has pointed out, etc.
1.8 *him* – who? – the farmer
1.8 *the Ministry* – as before
1.9 *an earlier statute* – earlier than what statute? – earlier than the Wildlife and Countryside Act
1.13 *having done so* – done what? – designated suitable areas, etc.
1.13 *it* – what? – The National Conservancy Council
1.14 *the occupier* – what occupier? – the occupier of the site
1.14 *but* – despite what? – despite the NCC's power to designate, etc.
1.15 *the encounters* – what encounters? – the negotiations between the NCC and the occupiers
1.17 *the Council* – what Council? – the NCC
1.17 *itself* – what's self? – the Council's
1.18 *it* – what? – the NCC
1.19 *the 'owner'* – what owner? – the owner of the site
1.20 *his, he, his* – who, whose? – the owner/ owner's
1.21 *but* – despite what? – despite what has just been said
1.22 *the farmer* – probably not anaphoric, i.e. it means 'farmers'
1.23 *he* – who? – the farmer
1.23 *larger* – larger than what? – larger than the 'body' consisting of the owner himself
11.28–9 *the private* – the private what? – the private interest
1.29 *this* – what? – the weighing of public interest against private interest
1.30 *it* – what? – the weighing of public interest, etc.
1.33 *another* – another what? – another part of the environment; – other than what? – other than the one just mentioned, namely the town
1.33 *such protection* – such as what? – such as the protection that would be extended, etc.

Chapter 3   Verbs and verb phrases

1   *(p. 49)*

The verbs are:
listen, suppose, leave, stand, blink, creak, scatter, and *promise.*

2   *(p. 49)*

a new situation develops (*present*); a well-known local farmer died (*past*); the lights shine (*present*); everybody left (*past*).

3   *(p. 49)*

The subjects are in italics: he swayed; *he* walked; *the camel at the zoo* sways; *it* walks; *The camel* despises; *the camel* is; *the camel* sees; *the great jeweller . . .* swung; *he* reached; *he* strode; *the four men* stood.

4   *(p. 50)*

base form	s-form	d-form	n-form	ing-form
REGULAR				
sway	sways	swayed	swayed	swaying
walk	walks	walked	walked	walking
despise	despises	despised	despised	despising
reach	reaches	reached	reached	reaching
IRREGULAR				
see	sees	saw	seen	seeing
swing	swings	swung	swung	swinging
stride	strides	strode	stridden	striding
stand	stands	stood	stood	standing

5   *(p. 50)*

1   I got; I found; the hurricane had knocked; I rigged; I had fixed; I hoisted; I went.

Elliptical ones hoisted; secured; went; filled; cast.

2   knew *d-form, irregular* (know)
happening *ing-form, regular* (happen)
started *d-form, regular* (start)
jerking *ing-form, regular* (jerk)
decided *d-form, regular* (decide)
met *d-form, irregular* (meet)
coming *ing-form, irregular* (come)
received *d-form, regular* (receive)
continued *d-form, regular* (continue)
banging *ing-form, regular* (bang)
getting *ing-form, irregular* (get)
jammed *d-form, regular* (jam)
hit *d-form,* irregular (hit)
bursted *d-form, regular* (burst) (*NB   In standard English this verb is irregular: d-form =* burst.)
allowing *ing-form, regular* (allow)
spill *base form, irregular* (*d-form =* spilt) *or regular* (*d-form =* spilled)
started *d-form, regular* (start)
landed *d-form, regular* (land)
have *base form, irregular*
lost *n-form, irregular* (lose)
let *d-form, irregular* (let)
go *base form, irregular*
came *d-form, irregular* (come)
giving *ing-form, irregular* (give)
putting *ing-form, irregular* (put)
request *base form, regular*

Irregular verbs

base form	s-form	d-form	n-form	ing-form
know	knows	knew	known	knowing
meet	meets	met	met	meeting
come	comes	came	come	coming
get	gets	got	got	getting
hit	hits	hit	hit	hitting
burst	bursts	burst	burst	bursting
spill	spills	spilt	spilt	spilling
have	has	had	had	having
lose	loses	lost	lost	losing
let	lets	let	let	letting
go	goes	went	gone	going
give	gives	gave	given	giving
put	puts	put	put	putting

6 (p. 51)

1.1a present perfect   *have given*
  1b present continuous   *are giving*
  2   present   *gives*
    present perfect continuous   *has been giving*
    present continuous   *is giving*
  3a past   *gave*
    past perfect   *had given*
  3b past continuous   *was giving*
                           were giving
  2a present perfect; *b* past; *c* past continuous; *d* present perfect continuous; *e* past perfect continuous.

7 (p. 51)

modal present perfect continuous   *may have been growing*
modal present continuous   *may be growing*
modal past perfect   *might have grown*
modal past continuous   *might be growing*

8 (p. 51)

found (*finite, past, cf.* finds); have . . . seen (*finite, present, cf.* had . . . seen); being (*non-finite*); to arrive (*non-finite*); are asking (*finite, present, cf.* were asking); having tried – to contact (*non-finite for both*); may be flying (*finite, present, cf.* might); was . . . flying (*finite, past, cf.* is . . . flying); having been flying (*non-finite*).

9 (p. 51)

jerking me off the ground (line 20–1): The barrel jerked me off the ground.
banging my head against the beam (line 25): I banged my head against the beam.
getting my fingers jammed in the pulley (line 25–6): I got my fingers jammed in the pulley.
allowing all the bricks to spill out (line 28): The barrel allowed all the bricks to spill out.

getting several painful cuts from the sharp edges (lines 33–4): I got several painful cuts from the sharp edges.
giving me another heavy blow on the head (lines 37–8): The barrel gave me another heavy blow on the head.
putting me in hospital (line 38): The barrel put me in hospital.

10 (p. 51)

Here are a sentence or two analysed as an example:

The Boundary Commission's counsel admitted in the High Court yesterday that the English Commissioners could have produced more equality between the electorates of the new parliamentary constituencies which they have proposed.

Mr John Melville Williams, QC, representing Mr Michael Foot and three other leaders of the Labour Party, described the statement as an important concession. 'We have been waiting for four months to hear this', he added.

Only finite verbs with subjects are relevant. These are:

The Boundary Commission's counsel admitted . . . (past tense; not the verb *be*; no agreement).
The English Commissioners could have produced (past tense of modal verb, no agreement).
. . . *they have proposed* (present tense; change of subject to third person singular requires different agreement: i.e. *he has proposed*).
Mr J. M. W. . . . described (past tense; not *be*; no agreement).
We have been waiting (present tense; change of subject to third person singular requires different agreement, e.g. *He has been waiting*).
. . . *he added* (past tense; not *be*; no agreement).

It can be seen that in only two out of the six cases is there potential variation to show agreement with the subject; the others would not change whatever the subject.

11　(p. 52)

Infinitives　to put; to destroy; to approach; to have; to designate; to do; to be; to be; to be.
Prepositional phrases　to the environmental impact; to a much larger body of interested persons; to another; to the disappearing beauties of the English landscape.

12　(p. 52)

Here are some samples:

He keeps arguing with me. (arguing: *ing-form*)
They have tried to fix a new shelf. (to fix: *to-infinitive*)
They have tried fixing a new shelf. (*ing-form*)
The manager has begun sending out memos. (*ing-form*)
The manager has begun to send out memos. (*to-infinitive*)
Those students finished reading it last week. (*ing-form*)
We managed to find a better one. (*to-infinitive*)
She likes climbing trees. (*ing-form*)
She would like to climb a tree. (*to-infinitive*)
I didn't mean to offend you. (*to-infinitive*)
He is pretending to be asleep. (*to-infinitive*)
The committee has agreed to donate some money. (*to-infinitive*)

13　(p. 52)

made up; turned out; coming down (tomorrow).

14　(p. 52)

rigged up (*complement* = a beam); hoisted up (*comp.* = a couple of barrels of bricks); hoisted . . . up (*comp.* = the barrel); went up (*no comp.*); cast off (*comp.* = the line); started down (*no comp.*); to hang on (*no comp.*); coming down (*no comp.*); to spill out (*no comp.*); coming up (*no comp.*); came down (*no comp.*).

15　(p. 52)

Here are some samples:

They are going to put me up for the night.
Shall I wash out these cups?
He wrote down the address.
Hear me out!
They always light up at about this time.
The militant group has split off.

16　(p. 52)

approached (*participants*: he, the Ministry of Agriculture)
gave (*participants*: the Ministry, him, a substantial grant)
negotiates . . . with (*participants*: the Council, the occupier)
is (*participant*: the farmer; *attribute*: a trustee)
will make (*participants*: they, a fundamental change)
weigh . . . against (*participants*: they, the public interest, the private (interest))
involves (*participants*: this, a growth of bureaucracy)
appear (*participant*: such people; *attribute*: powerless)
suffered (*participant*: the public interest)

2 Here are some samples:

He has lent me his tennis racket (*participants*: he, me, his tennis racket).
The mayoress has launched the new vessel (*ptnts*: the mayoress, the new vessel).
The workmen attached a new guttering to the old one (*ptnts*: the workmen, a new guttering, the old one).
Several advantages attach to this scheme (*ptnts*: several advantages, this scheme).
Our committee has combined with theirs (*ptnts*: our committee, theirs).
The management have combined our department with this one (*ptnts*: the management, our dept., this one).
He spoke for a long time (*ptnt*: he).
He spoke to me (*ptnts*: he, me).

The hostess uttered a few words of welcome (*ptnts*: the hostess, a few words of welcome).

The correspondent is writing us a long article.

The correspondent is writing a long article for us (*ptnts*: the correspondent, us, a long article).

These new pens write beautifully (*ptnt*: these new pens).

This car drives very smoothly (*ptnt*: this car).

She will drive my car tomorrow (*ptnts*: she, my car).

The handle broke (*ptnt*: the handle).

You have broken the handle (*ptnts*: you, the handle).

Children sleep very deeply (*ptnt*: children).

17 (p. 53)

Dynamic . . . went up the hill; . . . sold Henry her old Ford; . . . is getting hungry; . . . happened yesterday; . . . slams the door.

Stative . . . owned the old Ford; . . . is in the garage; . . . is hungry; . . . still seems serviceable; . . . stands; . . . looks modern; . . . seems disappointed; . . . is the Lord Mayor.

18 (p. 53)

diverse, *particular* (noun or adjective), *agree*, *sign* (noun or verb) *soft*, *danger* (noun), *symbol* (noun).

19 (p. 53)

Here are some of the possible verbs:

visualize (*cf.* visual); finalize (*cf.* final); synchronize (*no* *synchron, *but cf.* synchrony); mobilize (*no* *mobil, *but cf.* mobile); characterize (*cf.* character); realize (*cf.* real); jeopardize (*no* *jeopard, *but cf.* jeopardy); standardize (*cf.* standard); maximize (*not derived from maxim*, *but cf.* maximum); pressurize (*cf.* pressure); systematize (*no* *systemat, *but cf.* systematic); rationalize (*cf.* rational).

NB Words like *supervise* do not count since they are constructed: *super* + *vise* not *superv* + *ise*.

20 (p. 53)

The phrase (*n.*) is three words long.

They are going to exercise (*v.*) the troops.

Will you file (*v.*) these papers please?

The cooks (*n.*) have roasted the turkey.

The line branches (*v.*) at Didcot.

I am trying to sleep (*v.*)

They say (*v.*) that he may place (*v.*) a bet tomorrow.

The commands (*n.*) were given over the telephone.

She posts (*v.*) her letters on the way to work.

He never papers (*v.*) the front room.

21 (p. 53)

The slope (*n.*) is rather steep.

The roads slope (*v.*) downwards.

I have removed the cover (*n.*)

Please cover the table (*v.*).

His mind (*n.*) is very alert.

We don't mind (*v.*) the expense.

I can't remember your name (*n.*).

They are going to name (*v.*) the baby Harriet.

That step (*n.*) is terribly dangerous.

We always step (*v.*) over the wall.

I am looking forward to a change (*n.*).

Are you going to change (*v.*) the wording?

22 (p. 53)

For most speakers the words are stressed as follows:

discóunt (*v.*)
díscount (*n.*)
dischárge (*v.*)
díscharge (*n.*)

disguíse (*v. or n.*)
dismáy (*v. or n.*)
disgúst (*v. or n.*)
dislíke (*v. or n.*)
disgráce (*v. or n.*)

dispúte (*v.*)

When *dispute* is used as a noun very many speakers now stress it like *díscount*, and *discharge*, though the older usage is to stress it the same as the verb.

23   (p. 53)

The following have variable stress *object*, *progress*, *project*, *reject*, *conflict*, and (for some speakers) *decoy* and *research*. On the other hand *display*, *mistake*, *repair* and *concern* have fixed stress; for some speakers *decoy* and *research* belong to this group.

Chapter 4   Adjectives and adjective phrases

1   (p. 67)

The most obvious ones (though they do not all make sense in each context) are *is*, *tastes*, *smells*, *looks*, *sounds*, *seems*, *appears*. (The forms of the verbs have to be adjusted, of course, for agreement: *are*, *taste*, etc. They could also be in the past tense: *was*, *tasted*, etc.)

2   (p. 67)

very, rather, quite, somewhat, terribly, exceedingly, amazingly, terrifically, pretty, unbelievably, extraordinarily, extremely, really, surprisingly, etc.

3   (p. 67)

The inflectable ones are hard, lively, pure, clever, small, light, free, dirty, hollow, harsh, sound, dear, tall, cloudy, rusty, friendly, close, far (*irregular*: further, furthest, *or* farther, farthest), near.

4   (p. 67)

The following would be most likely to be inflectable, either because they do not appear to be derived or because, though derived, they appear to have the suffix *-ly* or *-y*: *pesh*, *omply*, *jite*, *osty*, *horge*, *baint*.

On the other hand, *regicaler* and *sirterousest*, etc. (like **musicaler*, **blusterousest*) would be ruled out because they do not conform to the conventional patterns of the language.

5   (p. 67)

To test which one is neutral, formulate the *How?* question: e.g. *How deep is it?* (The neutral one is in italics.)
deep/shallow; *wide*/narrow; *clean*/dirty; *good*/bad; *tight*/loose; *old*/young; *light*/dark; *heavy*/light; *ripe*/unripe

6   (p. 67)

Colour   *shocking pink, deep purple, light grey, brick red.*
Qualitative   *very green* (the greenness of the valley is more to do with its vegetation and beauty than with its colour); similarly with *marvellously blue*; *black* could be modified to give *a very black mood*, but not *a jet black mood*; we can have *a rather grey area*, but not *a pale grey area*.

7   (p. 67)

Qualitative   costly, splendid, natural, important, dreamlike, matter-of-fact, young.
Colour   none.
Classifying   Chinese, bureaucratic, public, visual, black.

8   (p. 68)

1   distracting signals; corrupting literature; crushing blows; amusing lyrics.
2   existing procedures; flowering bulbs; winning side; tinkling cymbal; invading forces; lying stories; rising tide; bulging eyes.
3   giving evidence; forging papers; awaiting burial; escaping detection; reclaiming prisoners; taking exercise.

9 (p. 68)

Here are some possible answers:

I can smell burning toast.
I left him burning toast.
Breaking windows are a hazard.
They enjoy breaking windows.
These seem infuriating monkeys.
Infuriating monkeys is cruel.
Examining magistrates were usually sympathetic.
Examining magistrates was tiresome.

10 (p. 68)

When a determiner is put into a noun phrase, it marks the beginning of the phrase; if the ing-form is included in the noun phrase, it has to follow the determiner. Hence *burning some toast* can only be a verb followed by a noun phrase acting as complement, while *some burning toast* can only be a noun phrase. Similarly with *an examining magistrate* and *examining a magistrate*. The third one, *understanding traffic*, cannot be interpreted like *some understanding traffic* since *traffic* cannot be the subject of the verb *understand* (*traffic which understands*); it must therefore be more like *understanding some traffic*, in which *some traffic* is the complement of the verb. Conversely, *children* can be the subject of *laugh* (*some laughing children* = *some children who laugh*), but cannot be the complement of the verb *laugh* (*We laughed some children*). The relation between *interest* and *books* must be one of subject to verb (*the books interest us*) and cannot be verb to complement (*something interests the books*).

11 (p. 68)

Verb + complement:

   ... *convicts the murderer*
   ... *paints the surface*

Subject + verb:

   the stones fall
   the light vanishes

12 (p. 68)

There is, of course, no final answer to this exercise. Here are some possible answers:

Jane is good at making coffee.
Penelope is delighted with her new job.
She would have been so inefficient that it would have merited dismissal.
He was too angry to speak to the people who had been absent.

13 (p. 68)

easy events to photograph; suitable material for the purpose; *a longer car than the trailer; better health than mine; *glad people of your help; an unreasonable man about getting time off; *a liable type of car to heavy running costs; the longest river in this part of the country; a comfortable chair for sitting at table; *an uncertain organizer of his aims.

14 (p. 69)

Again there is no final answer, but the following are possible:

It is a dangerous roof to walk on: The roof is dangerous to walk on.
It was an alarming scene to witness: The scene was alarming to witness.
They are important facts to know about: The facts are important to know about.
They are useful people to meet: The people are useful to meet.
This is an easy garden to look after: This garden is easy to look after.
These are boring programmes to watch: These programmes are boring to watch.
They were thoughtless words to say: *The words were thoughtless to say.
This is a laborious hill to climb: This hill is laborious to climb.
They were ineffective measures to take: *The measures were ineffective to take.
These are harmful leaves to touch: The leaves are harmful to touch.

This is a difficult typewriter to use: This typewriter is difficult to use.

This is a big house to keep warm: This house is big to keep warm.

This is a permissible door to open: *This door is permissible to open.

15 (p. 69)

Gradable timid, substantial, earlier, suitable, special, decorous, major, obvious, larger, fundamental, vast, antisocial, powerless.

Ungradable public (*occurring several times*), economic, environmental, national, scientific, rare, answerable, interested, listed, private, existing, disappearing, English.

(In this context whether an orchid is rare is a matter of definition; similarly a person is either answerable or not answerable in law, and an interested party is not somebody whose attention is engaged, but somebody who stands to gain.)

16 (p. 69)

In passages of about this length from the *Guardian*, I found:

arts criticism adjectives adjectives, including eleven gradable (i.e. *c.* 73 per cent);

current affairs reporting seventeen adjectives, including two gradable and possibly one other doubtful one (i.e. 18 per cent at most).

17 (p. 69)

Irish-type Spanish, Chinese, French, Swedish, Portuguese, Swiss.

American-type German, Norwegian, Russian, Australian.

18 (p. 69)

If you used the *Oxford English Dictionary* (*OED*) you may have made some surprising discoveries. The ones that are not in *Collins'* *English Dictionary* (1979) are marked *; those not in the *OED* are marked **.

easeful is rare (it occurs in Keats, '. . . half in love with easeful death'); *easy* has a slightly different meaning.

mindful.

**causeful* seems not to be used much nowadays, but the *OED* quotes a writer of 1849: '. . . more causeful of blood and tears than . . .'.

fanciful.

**sightful* is also rare or obsolete; the *OED* has some sixteenth- and seventeenth-century instances, e.g. '. . . the understanding groweth more sharp and sightful' (1594); cf. *sighted*.

deceitful.

***solaceful* there seems to be no alternative adjective based on *solace*.

**faultful* The *OED* quotes Ruskin (1858): '. . . the limiting lines between virtuous contentment and faultful carelessness'; cf. *faulty*.

***trashful* cf. *trashy*.

wasteful.

***symbolful* cf. *symbolic*.

insightful.

19 (p. 69)

taste (*n.*), tasty; flavour (*n*), flavoursome; thought (*n.*), thoughtful, thoughtless; reason (*n.*), reasonable; logic, (*n.*), logical; concept (*n.*), conceptual; theory (*n.*), theoretic, theoretical; imagine (*v.*), imaginary, imaginative; soap (*n.*), soapy; explode (*v.*), explosive; problem (*n.*), problematic, problematical; historic (*adj.*), historical; wife (*n.*), wifely; tyrant (*n.*), tyrannical, tyrannous; statue (*n.*), statuesque; accent (*n. and v.*), accented, accentual; satire (*n.*), satiric, satirical; govern (*v.*), governable; fame (*n*), famous; sincerity (*n.*), sincere; saltiness (*n.*), salty, salt; weep (*v.*), weepy; truth (*n.*), true, truthful; respect (*n. and v.*), respectful, respectable, respective; legalize (*v.*), legal; widen (*v.*), wide; shame (*n. and v.*), shameful, shameless; virtue (*n*), virtuous, ?virtual; hunger (*n.*), hungry; custody (*n.*), custodial; trouble (*n. and v.*), troublesome, troublefree.

20 (p. 70)

The	A welcome	that	B please-	s	C bring-	s	the	D pious	E answer
	answer		answer		answer			daily	welcome
	cause		arrive		cause			outstanding	cause
	pilgrim		dwindle		lose			prolific	pilgrim
	secret		emerge		manage			recent	secret
	show		lose		provide			secret	show
	song		?save		save			original	song
			show		show				
			take		take				
	1		**2a**		**2b**			**3**	**1**

Class 1   noun
Class 2   verb; *a* intransitive; *b* transitive
Class 3   adjective

No passive possible for: He got impatient, You must not swear, The trouble is beginning, The food is in the kitchen, The floor is yours, I'm going home.

Chapter 5 Sentences

1 (p. 86)

The notices are written (by somebody).
Some telephone calls are being expected (by them).
The expedition was soon forgotten (by the public).
Every request was dismissed (by his employers).
She was tormented (by terrible dreams).
I have been invited (by my friends).
The walking stick had been taken (by Charles).
The lamp was being trimmed (by her).

2 (p. 86)

Passive sentences

It will be kept (by him).
The pudding had better be warmed (by me).
She was taken away (by them).
The luggage has been brought to her (by them).
I was told (by the landlord).

3 (p. 87)

John told a story to the children.
The children were told a story.
A story was told to the children.
That woman is buying some clothes for Daphne.
Daphne is being bought some clothes (by that woman).
Some clothes are being bought for Daphne (by that woman).
I'm digging a hole for you.
You are being dug a hole (by me).
A hole is being dug for you (by me).
The management won't grant any more holiday to us.
We won't be granted any more holiday (by the management).
No more holiday will be granted to us (by the management).
They have sold a lot of rubbish to their customers.
Their customers have been sold a lot of rubbish (by them).

A lot of rubbish has been sold to their customers (by them).

Mary is lending the car to the neighbours.

The neighbours are being lent the car (by Mary).

The car is being lent to the neighbours (by Mary).

She is lending it to them.

They are being lent it (by her).

It is being lent to them (by her).

4   (p. 87)

Type 3

He was telling me the reason.

The boy threw the harbour master a rope.

My father left us a large fortune.

You owe me quite a few meals.

They are making me a suit.

We may find you some more work.

The shop is saving you a copy.

Type 4

They left me depressed.

The board considered her competent.

They make you welcome.

He called her a liar.

The public think him insincere.

We all found them helpful.

The committee will declare the application void.

5   (p. 87)

Type 1   4, 7 (*miserably* = adjunct)
Type 2   2
Type 3   6, 9
Type 4   1, 8 (*at present* = adjunct), 12
Type 5   5, 11
Type 6   3, 10 (*after two hours* = adjunct)

6   (p. 87)

1 Every movement	expresses	her furious resolution
subject	verb	object

2 She	's done	it	at the first shot
subj.	verb	obj.	adjunct

3 Nearly everybody else in the cast	had learnt	their lines
subject	verb	obj.

4 The jury's decision	was	a just solution to the case
subject	verb	complement

5 The man from the office	read	us	a very short message	in a stifled voice
subject	verb	ind. obj.	dir. obj.	adjunct

7   (p. 87)

Declarative   1, 5, 13
Yes–no interrogative   2, 9, 14
Alternative interrogative   3, 12
WH-interrogative   4, 6, 8, 10
Imperative   7, 11

8   (p. 88)

Passive   4, 5, 7, 8, 9
Active   1, 2, 3, 6

9   (p. 88)

This knowledge	he	had used
object	subj.	verb

On his success	could depend	their morale
place comp.	verb	subject

Other pigs	you	couldn't go	near
object of preposition	subj.	verb	preposition

The latter	he	divides	as follows
object	subj.	verb	adjunct

Over there	live	my parents
place comp.	verb	subject

His crimes	he	kept	secret
object	subj.	verb	comp.

10 (p. 88)

1 adjunct; 2 complement; 3 post-modifier; 4 post-modifier; 5 subject; 6 complement; 7 adjunct; 8 subject ... complement; 9 post-modifier.

11 (p. 88)

This key will only give a few hints at the linguistic categories involved in a possible answer. It is up to you to assess your own literary appreciation.

1 *Person*   the title of the poem and the poem itself are supposed to be spoken by different people, to each other. Thus first and second person reference get reversed.

After the title, the poem begins in a third person narrative mode; first and second person are then re-introduced in stanzas four and five.

2 *Mood*   the majority of the clauses are declarative, as would be expected in a narrative. Stanzas four and five, however, have three imperatives: ... *come*; ... *review your sentence*; ... *give me four hundred years ...*, and a yes–no interrogative: *Can rage be so intense?* (a rhetorical question deprecating the lover's rage). All this implies the immediate presence of an addressee. (Note also the use of a noun phrase in vocative function: *my angry love*.) There is a discrepancy here, since the reader of the poem is not likely to be the poet's 'love' – there are two 'layers' of addressee-ship!

The declarative mood of the opening sentences is somewhat modified by the use of the adverb *surely* (expressing a meaning such as 'this must be the oldest'), and by the parenthetical clauses: *old wives affirm, annalists agree* (suggesting 'it is not me that says this').

Index